ARISTARHOS M.

Speechless
in Greece?
No thanks!

ATHENS 2003

© Copyright 2003   MICHAEL TOUBIS PUBLICATIONS S.A.
Nisiza Karela, Koropi, Attiki
Telephone: +30 210 6029974, Fax: +30 210 6646856
Web Site: http://www.toubis.gr

ISBN: 960-540-464-8

ACKNOWLEDGEMENTS

The writing of this phrase book was
a mosaic of several people's ideas, suggestions,
and corrections. Special thanks go to Joe Compton,
Pam Glowacki, Despina Matsouka, Candice Pettifer
and Charlotte Reid; also to Kelly Nika for the computer
help of earlier drafts. Fanis Skafidas has put life
in this phrase book with cartoons and symbols
most amusing and fun. Last but not least,
thanks to George Dimopoulos, my editor at Toubis.
"Speechless in Greece? No, thanks!" is dedicated
to my "mitera" for her frequent discussions
about language.

Speechless in Greece? No, thanks!

- Teach yourself Greek visually!
- Survival language tactics!
- Fit for Greece!
- Greek at a glance!
- An unusual phrase book!
- Read less, learn more!
- A "stressless" approach!
- A cultural guide too!

Table of Contents

I. First things first 8

A. Not everybody speaks English!
How about Greek? 10
B. How can I use this book? No problem!
Follow steps 1-2-3... ready! 12
C. Standardized format for fast access!
This is really what I need! 14

II. Transliteration 16

A. Transliteration: What's that? 18
B. Do I really have to be able to read Greek
to say "hello"? 20

III. The three kits 22

A. Survival Kit (...the first twelve units) 24
B. Essential Kit (...the next twelve units) 50
C. Necessary Kit (...the last twelve units) 76

IV. The cultural guide 102

A. Where to go! 104
B. What to buy! 106
C. How to understand! 108
D. Who to contact! 110
E. Why bother? 112

V. Do you know your ABC's? 114

A. The Greek alphabet. 116
B. Some grammar rules. 118

VI. Glossaries 120

A. Greek – English glossary 122
B. English – Greek glossary 144

VII. Further reading 162

A. www: Are you connected?
So much the better! 164
B. Books, etc... 166

First
things
first

I First things first

This section is a short introduction about the language we want to learn, namely Greek. It will also guide you on how to make the best possible use of this book. Finally, it will present the format used and highlight the symbols found throughout the book.

A

Not everybody speaks English!
How about Greek?

B

How can I use this book?
No problem!
Follow steps 1-2-3... ready!

C

Simple format for fast access!
This is what I really need!

A Not everybody speaks English! How about Greek?

It is hard to believe that not everybody will speak English to us but the latest census research has shown that there are 350,000,000 native speakers and about 650,000,000 who have learned English as a second or foreign language. That leaves us with about five billion people (!!!) who cannot speak English to us. That's a lot of people to disregard, don' t you think?

This realization becomes even more intense especially when traveling to small villages or remote foreign places. Greece is not an exception to this rule. You will definitely encounter many people who will try to employ their varying English language skills at all different levels. However, in some situations knowing and using some Greek may be helpful. Greeks will also welcome such an effort on your part and that can make all the difference in your contacts. You will realize that they will quickly warm to you if you *try to speak Greek to them.*

The Modern Greek language is spoken - in its standard form (standard Modern Greek) - in Greece,

Cyprus, and the substantial Greek Diaspora (USA, Australia, Canada, Germany). Of course, there are small Greek communities in several other parts of the world including South Africa, South America, and continental Europe, particularly southern Italy. At the turn of the century, approximately 13,500,000 *spoke* Greek as their first language with about 10,000,000 alone in Greece. There are also many who have learned Greek either by studying or living and working in Greece.

How about Greek?

The evolution of the language dates back 4,000 years. Ancient Greek had three main dialects: Ionian (spoken in Asia Minor and on many Aegean islands), Doric (spoken in the Peloponnese), and Attic (spoken in the Greater Athens area). Attic became the dominant dialect at the time of Alexander the Great around 330 BC. An idiom known as "Koine" derived from the Attic dialect and Modern Greek developed from that "Koine" idiom. Over the centuries Modern Greek has retained much of the *vocabulary* of Ancient Greek but differs from it considerably in grammar and pronunciation. Modern Greek has absorbed many foreign words particularly from Turkish, Slavic, and Italian, obviously its immediate neighbors, but has itself contributed to many languages including English.

4.000 years of language history!

Also check Unit 5

B How can I use this book?
No problem!
Follow Steps 1-2-3... ready!

The triple-s approach.

The idea behind the triple-s approach

Steps 1-2-3 ...ready!

Do you really want to know how to use this book? That's easy! Simply read the suggestions and comments that follow. This phrase book will help you to make your first steps at being understood in many different situations you will encounter with Greek speakers in Greece or abroad. It is based on what we would like to term as "the triple-s" approach. The triple-s derives from *"Show - See - or - Say"*!
Not bad, right?

The idea is that many people like yourself would like to be able to communicate at any elementary level with Greeks by *showing* some words found as visual clues throughout the thirty six units, by understanding a few everyday words and expressions when uttered by Greeks, and of course by saying a few things yourself in Greek.

■ Step 1: *"Let me show you what I mean!"* is the first step you can employ with all visual clues and prompts found in this phrase book. This simply means that you don't have to learn the whole phrase book by heart, which wouldn't be fun anyway! Instead, become familiar with the parts of this book so you easily know where to look up what when the necessity arises!

step 1

■ Step 2: *"Oh, I see what you are saying!"* is the second step you can employ with materials you feel confident following and understanding like greetings, everyday expressions, directions, or suggestions Greeks use with you in conversations. Many units include a special section titled "Watch out for it!" which groups important useful words and phrases that you could pick up while listening and trying to tune into Greek.

step 2

■ Step 3: *"Wow, I can actually say quite a few things in Greek!"* We don't want to overemphasize the importance of this step, as pointed in the previous section. What we want to do here is to remind you of the title of this phrase book and make you ready for the phrase: "Speechless in Greece? Who me? No, thanks!"

step 3

Voila! There is no magic behind these steps. Feel free to use any possible combination of *steps 1-2-3* when meeting Greeks and have fun! Your efforts will give you an unforgettable experience. Don't miss out!

C Standardized format for fast access! This is what I really need!

Each unit is presented on only two opposite pages!

You will soon realize that there is a simple and standardized format used throughout this phrase book. All different parts and sections including the 36 units of this phrase book are each presented on only two opposite pages! This is true for everything except the two glossaries at the back of the phrase book, which for obvious reasons could not fit on two single opposite pages. By doing so, we believe that you can become easily familiar with the materials covered in this phrase book, navigate yourself through and access anything fast! If this sounds good, read on.

At a glance!

Another feature of this phrase book is that it guides you throughout with several visual clues and prompts, thus making all presentations easy and fun. In addition, these visual clues and prompts assist you in boosting memory retention. Everybody knows and acknowledges that "a picture is worth a thousand words"!

What can I find in each unit?

The simple format is further developed in each unit which usually contains some of the following:

1 TABLES - CHARTS

These include word-banks usually in alphabetical order related to each topic.

2 VISUAL CLUES - PROMPTS

Every possible effort has been made to visually represent key words and ideas.

3 PHRASES - EXPRESSIONS

These include the most useful phrases and expressions necessary for each topic.

4 SYMBOLS

These following symbols guide you in an easy and fun way to access the right information fast.

What does this symbol mean?

TIPS AND TRICKS!

Simple explanations for survival tactics in Greece.

DOUBLE CHECK!

Cross referencing materials and additional information in different units.

WATCH OUT FOR!

The P's and Q's in Greek and what to tune in to.

FAQ AND INFOPACK!

Useful information on frequently asked questions in everyday topics.

TICK MARK!

Try to memorize most of the materials with the check symbol.

AT A GLANCE!

Summarized information presented visually.

FINALLY WIRED!

Internet addresses for further information.

Transliteration

Transliteration

This section includes explanations and examples about the transliteration system used throughout this phrase book. It points out its validity but also its shortcomings and guides the learner on how to say a few things in Greek without being intimidated by the Greek alphabet.

A Transliteration:
What's that?

B Do I really have to be able to read Greek to simply say "hello"?

Transliteration:
What's that?

Transliteration is a system that attempts to represent Greek sounds using a western alphabet! It is a close phonetic representation of how Greek words sound in an English script. Let's look at an example: Unit 1 deals with the Greek word "γεια σου" for hello! Is it easier for you to read the word γεια σου or [yásu]? It is generally known that many people feel intimidated with the new script, and many give up after some time. Contrary to popular opinion though, Greek is not a difficult language to speak, particularly at a beginner's level. So our above example might frighten you as a spelling but not as a sound! Right? And this book wants you to break the ice and say a few things in Greek but not necessarily write them!

Where will you find transliteration? Nowhere! Or almost nowhere! Only in a few language books like this one and actually in many different forms and shapes! Greek unlike other languages which use a standardized transliteration system including Korean, Japanese, and Chinese, has not established *an accepted standardized system* yet! This creates a special problem though because the sound of "hello" could have been transliterated also as "yássou", "yiásu", or even "giásou"! And somehow all versions may be partially correct! Unfortunately, there is no right answer to this issue yet, but hopefully most of our readers will have no trouble with the transliteration system we have devised!

The transliteration of Greek into English though poses a problem to the Greek authorities who have trouble spelling the names of streets, towns, rivers, mountains etc! So, do not be surprised if you see some names spelled differently on a map or on a signpost! Athens for instance has been transliterated on sign posts as ATHINA or ATHINAI. The spelling of Greek names in passports also causes serious difficulties. One example is the name George which shows up in English as Yiorghos, Georghios, Georgios, or even Gheoryios! Last names are even worse! In the same family, one member was TSOUKAS, the second one TSUKAS, and the third TSOUCAS!

Sould we skip transliteration after all? No! Apart from its shortcomings, its value, especially in assisting reading at early stages, has been generally accepted. Many learners increased their tempo and pace, left intimidating thoughts behind and enjoyed their Greek with or without an accent!

I can't find it on my map! Try an alternative spelling!

B Do I really have to be able to read Greek to simply say "hello"???

No! The Greek alphabet, as stated in the previous section, is intimidating for many learners but apart from its challenges we believe it is easy to pronounce most Greek words. What we have done below for you is to give you some tips and ideas on how to understand the transliteration system we use and how to read words and phrases in their transliterated form as found in this phrase book.

Read the alphabet on page 116.

Try to read the following notes in parallel to the section on the Greek alphabet found on page 116. Both sections will give you a better picture of all the Greek letters and the sounds they produce. Keep in mind that the transliteration system is an *approximate phonetic representation* of Greek words and cannot replace native speakers uttering those words.

Good to know!

In our transliteration system both individual letters and two-letter combinations have been used. *The individual letters used are:* [a-b-d-e-f-g-h-i-k-l-m-n-o-p-r-s-t-u-v-x-y-z]. If you compare this list with the English alphabet you will realize four letters are missing. Those are: [c-j-q-w]. This is simply because one transliteration represents the sound of more than one letter. For example, the sound for the initial letter in the words "cope-king-quote" is represented by the letter [k] for all three! *The two – letter combinations used are:* [af-av-ch-dh-dz-ef-ev-gh-mb-nd-nh-ng-ts]. From all these combinations only the [dh] cluster does not appear in English and it has been used to represent the sound "th" in "this" but not in "thin". The [gh] cluster represents the sound of the letter "y" in "yield" or even "w" in "woman" but not in "ghost".

In order to pronounce Greek words especially if they are long, you should break them down into smaller chunks or syllables as they're called in grammar. For instance, reading the word "hello" is like reading [yá-su] or [ka-li-mé-ra] for "good morning". Remember, that no syllable exists in Greek without a vowel sound. Thus, a word in Greek usually has as many syllables as it has vowels! There are usually four possible types of syllables in Greek: those including only one vowel, or one vowel and one consonant, or one vowel and two consonants, or one vowel and three consonants. Some examples from Unit 4 are: March [már-ti-os] May [má-i-os], June [i-ú-ni-os], fall [fthi-nó-po-ro]. The accent mark shows you where to stress more. Practice will make you more familiar.

Greek has five vowel sounds: [a - e - i - o - u].

Whenever in doubt, ask a Greek how a word sounds.

The
three
kits

The three kits

ABC is all you need! This section is developed for most everyday situations you are likely to encounter while in Greece. It is divided into three parts of twelve units each. All units are independent and you can decide which one to read first; we do however suggest that you read the first twelve units first which will prepare you for a smoother transition to the other 24 units. The first 12 units will also give you an easy introduction into the Greek language, they will point out perhaps the most common words for you to use including greetings and farewells, and they will also highlight some unique Greek features. No matter what, have fun with one or another part of this section!

A The Survival Kit
(... the first twelve units...)

B The Essential Kit
(... the next twelve units...)

C The Necessary Kit
(... the last twelve units...)

A The Survival Kit

The first twelve units
can be used just before
your trip to Greece
or upon your arrival.

1 The *one*, single, most important Greek word!

2 Heads or tails? *Two* ways of saying "you" for you!

3 *Three*'s a company!

4 The *four* seasons by... Vivaldi
... and their corresponding months.

5 Can you think of any words of Greek
origin in the next *five* seconds?

6 Help! English anybody? The *six* most important
phrases to slow down Greeks!

7 *Seven* days in a week.

8 The *eight* most important greetings
and farewells.

9 *Nine* colors.

10 The numbers one to *ten* (1 - 10) for you!

11 Am I an actress yet? *Eleven* grimaces
and gestures to mimic... if you can!

12 *Twelve* hours later!

The one most important Greek word!

[ya] is perhaps the most important word in Greek! Even if you decide never to speak Greek γεια! [ya] is probably the single, most common word you will hear on several occasions in your visit or stay in Greece.

Don't hesitate to use it yourself as it will give you some pleasure and break the ice in this new endeavor! [ya] has more than one meaning depending on the situation and context that is used. Look at the cartoons below and check the different meanings.

γεια ! pronounced [ya] means :

a. "Cheers" ! while clinking glasses
   at a party,

b. "Hi! or Hello!" in informal situations,

c. "How do you do? - Hello!" when
   meeting people

d. "Goodbye! or So long!" and

e. "Bless you!" when somebody is sneezing!

Quite an important word, don't you think?

Tips and tricks !

The sound of [ya] and not its spelling
in Greek can formulate many important
Greek words as their first syllable.
To introduce some below :

[yatí]? why? (in questions)

[yatí] because (in statements)

[yalí] glass

[yayá] grandmother

It's much more important to be able
to know *where* to find what you want
to use in a specific situation rather than
trying to memorize big chunks. We are
almost sure you will not forget [ya] easily!

What... if I forget?

Unlike English, Greek uses two different "you" forms depending on the situation and whether formal or informal language is necessary. The two different forms are εσύ [esí] and εσείς [esís], something similar to "du" and "Sie" in German or "tu" and "Lei" in Italian, or even "tu" and "vous" in French!

This phrase book mostly uses the second form εσείς [esís] which is appropriate for addressing one person in formal situations or many people together.

Some examples illustrating this are:

>Εσείς είστε κύριε Σμιθ;
>[esís íste kírie Smith]?
>Is that *you* Mr. Smith?

and...

>Πού πάτε εσείς;
>[pu páte esís]?
>Where are *you* going?

or...

>Εσείς;
>[esís]?
>*You*? or How about *you*?

This affects mostly all phrases using a formal "you - form" assuming that it is more common in early introductions and first contacts in Greece. Naturally many Greeks will initiate the εσύ [esi] form quite early on in your meetings and providing that you feel comfortable with it *you can gradually switch over.*

When
to switch?

3 Three's a company!

[su] or [sas] ?

It is essential for you to understand and grasp the idea discussed in Unit 2, since it applies to several aspects of everyday language. One important application is with the word γεια [ya] which can also be heard as γεια σου! [yásu] or γεια σας! [yá sas].

*[ya],
[yá su],
and
[yá sas]*

[ya] is general without specifying whether you address someone *formally or informally*. In contrast, [yá su] is used in singular with a person we consider a friend or close to us and we do not need to use formal or polite language. [yá sas] on the other hand is formal when addressing one person we do not know well or in the plural for talking to more than one person.

This idea can be easily extrapolated and used on *several other occasions* with important words you will encounter in subsequent units. One example to illustrate this is the word καλημέρα! [kaliméra] which means Good morning!

[kaliméra]
generally means "good morning",

[kaliméra su]
"good morning to you",
when addressing
one person informally

and [kaliméra sas]
"good morning to you"
addressing many people
or one person formally.

Interesting and simple, right?

[kaliméra]!
Good morning!

4

The four seasons by...
Vivaldi... and their
corresponding months

*How cold is it
in Greece?
Also check
Unit 32.*

Many people visit Greece during the summer, since they come from colder climates. *Summer temperatures* can easily reach 30⁰-35⁰ C in the shade, which may be something to consider for those with breathing or heart problems. Also bear in mind that winters are mild especially in the south but many places are snowed in for days in the north. The table below gives you the average temperatures of three cities in central, northern, and southern Greece throughout the year.

*The degrees are
given
in both
centigrade
and Fahrenheit.*

	Athens	Thessalonica	Rhodes
January	13 - 55	4 - 40	15 - 60
February	15 - 60	10 - 50	17 - 65
March	17 - 65	13 - 55	21 - 70
April	21 - 70	17 - 65	23 - 75
May	23 - 75	21 - 70	26 - 80
June	29 - 85	26 - 80	32 - 90
July	32 - 90	29 - 85	34 - 95
August	36 - 95	32 - 90	36 - 100
September	26 - 80	26 - 80	32 - 90
October	21 - 70	17 - 65	29 - 85
November	16 - 60	10 - 50	21 - 70
December	10 - 50	4 - 40	16 - 60

Spring
[ánixi]
Άνοιξη

March	[mártios]	Μάρτιος
April	[aprílios]	Απρίλιος
May	[máios]	Μάιος

Summer
[kalokéri]
Καλοκαίρι

June	[iúnios]	Ιούνιος
July	[iúlios]	Ιούλιος
August	[ávghustos]	Αύγουστος

Fall
[fthinóporo]
Φθινόπωρο

September	[septémvrios]	Σεπτέμβριος
October	[októvrios]	Οκτώβριος
November	[noémvrios]	Νοέμβριος

Winter
[himónas]
Χειμώνας

December	[dhekémvrios]	Δεκέμβριος
January	[ianuários]	Ιανουάριος
February	[fevruários]	Φεβρουάριος

5 Can you think of any words of Greek origin in English in the next five seconds?

From Greek into English.

From English into Greek.

Many people fail tests. Especially when they are timed and naturally five seconds is not enough time for any real test. In your case though, we hope that you came up with a couple of words and you're indeed aware of the plethora of words of Greek origin found in English. Not only scientific medical jargon like "oncology" with "onco" meaning "tumor" in Greek, but also everyday, common words like *"idea", "music", or "program"*.

It is also very encouraging and you will be happily surprised to hear quite a few English words in a Greek context; to name a few: *"ferry boat", "tennis", or "football"*. You will also see several "W.C." and STOP signs written like that. And of course, you will hear on several occasions Greeks using the expression "OK!" to signify that everything is all right!

New technological terms have also been introduced in the everyday language; "computer", "fax", and "internet" are just some examples of the English used in Greek.

Below we provide you with a few words whose first part (prefix) will create an important list for you:

calligraphy	καλή [**kalí**]	good
cacophony	κακό [**kakó**]	bad
macroorganism	μακρό [**makró**]	big
microcamera	μικρό [**mikró**]	small
polyglot	πολύ [**polí**]	many
oligopoly	ολίγο [**olígho**]	a few
monopoly	μόνο [**móno**]	only

The second part of these words is also a basis for another list of important Greek words. Can you guess their meanings without looking them up below?

[grafí] writing, [foní] voice, [orghanizmós] organism, [kámera] camera, [ghlósa] language, and [póli-si] I sell.

Help! English anybody? The six most important phrases to slow down Greeks!

People always feel better if somebody can speak their mother tongue. Below are important phrases in emergency situations (when you actually want to slow down Greek speakers, to ask them if they speak English, etc.).

1. Slow down!

[sighá] Σιγά!
Slow Down!
Don't speak so fast!

2. Say it again!

[péste to xaná]
Πέστε το ξανά!
Say it again!
Can you repeat it?

[pos léne "water"
sta eliniká]?
Πώς λένε "water"
στα ελληνικά;
What is "water"
in Greek?

3. What is
"water"
in Greek?
[neró] is water
in Greek!

[dhen katalavéno]
Δεν καταλαβαίνω!
I don't understand!

4. I don't
understand!

[miláte angliká]?
Μιλάτε αγγλικά;
Do you speak
English?

5. Do you
speak English?

[ti]? [pos]?
[ti ípate]?
Τι; Πώς; Τι είπατε;
What? How?
What did you say?

6. What?
How? What
did you say?

What day
is today?
[ti mera ine
simera]?
Τι μέρα είναι
σήμερα?

We often lose track of what day
it is while on vacation. In Greece
this is not so bad, since time seems
to stand still at times if you
are not on a business trip under time
pressure. Below is a table of the
seven days of the week.

Monday	[dheftéra]	Δευτέρα
Tuesday	[tríti]	Τρίτη
Wednsday	[tetárti]	Τετάρτη
Thursday	[pémti]	Πέμπτη
Friday	[paraskeví]	Παρασκευή
Saturday	[sávato]	Σάββατο
Sunday	[kiriakí]	Κυριακή

!

The *words*
in brackets
have more
than one
possible ending.

Monday is the "second" day of the
week. [dhefter-] means "second". Similarly,
[trit-] means "third", [tetart-] means
"fourth", and [pemd-] means "fifth".
[paraskev-] stands for "prepare"
so Friday is "the day of preparation",
Saturday "the day of the Sabbath", and
Sunday "the day of the Lord" since [kiri-]
is the Lord!

The following seven days are
the most important public or religious
holidays in Greece:

*The seven
most important
public holidays
in Greece.*

Jan. 1
New Year's Day
[protohroniá]
Πρωτοχρονιά

Jan. 6
Epiphany
[theofánia]
Θεοφάνια

Mar. 25
Independence Day
[iméra anexartisías]
Ημέρα Ανεξαρτησίας

May 1
May Day
[protomayá]
Πρωτομαγιά

Aug. 15
Assumption Day
[i kímisi tis theotóku]
Η Κοίμηση της Θεοτόκου

Oct. 28
Entry into WW II
[ikostí oghdhói oktovríu]
Εικοστή ογδόη Οκτωβρίου

Dec. 25
Christmas Day
[hristúghena]
Χριστούγεννα.

*Also visit
Unit 4 for
the names
of the months.*

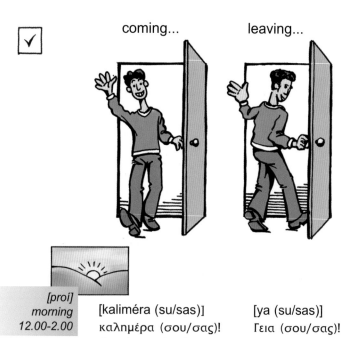

coming...   leaving...

[proí]
morning
12.00-2.00

[kaliméra (su/sas)]
καλημέρα (σου/σας)!
Good morning!

[ya (su/sas)]
Γεια (σου/σας)!
Bye

[mesiméri]
afternoon
2.00-4.00

[ya (su/sas)]
Γεια (σου/σας)!
Hello!

[kaló mesiméri]
Καλό μεσημέρι!
Have a nice
(early) afternoon!

[hérete]
Χαίρετε!
Good afternoon!

[kaló apóghevma]
Καλό απόγευμα!
Have a nice
(late) afternoon!

[apóghevma]
late
afternoon
4.00-6.00

[kalispéra (su/sas)]
Καλησπέρα (σου/σας)!
Good evening!

[kaliníhta (su/sas)]
Καληνύχτα (σου/σας)!
Good night!

[vrádhi]
evening
6.00-12.00

The usage of [su] and [sas] as discussed in unit 3 is useful here with many greetings and farewells.
The times are only rough indications. You might hear [kaliméra] at 2:00 o'clock in the afternoon or [yásu] at 10:00 in the morning! Especially [ya], [yásu], or [yásas] can be heard on several occasions throughout the day.

As a rule of thumb you can repeat the greeting you hear. You can do the same with the farewell [ya] or [kaliníhta] and you can use the word [epísis] επίσης meaning "likewise" or "the same to you" for [kaló mesiméri] and [kaló apóghevma]. Remember you can say [kaliméra] or [kaliméra su] addressing one person informally and [kaliméra sas] addressing many people or one person formally.

9 Nine colours.

Don't be afraid to write in this book. You can underline or highlight words or phrases important to you. By doing so, you will become more familiar with one part or another, and it will be easier to find information useful to you. Especially in this unit "black - and - white" are not very attractive colors for the following cartoons. Right? So, pull out your crayons and put some colors in your book!

[*fanári*] is traffic light in Greek!

. . . a traffic light is . . .

1. [portokalí] πορτοκαλί orange

2. [kókino] κόκκινο red

3. [prásino] πράσινο green

[*ílios*] is sun in Greek!

. . . the sun is . . .

4. [kírino] κίτρινο yellow

. . . salt and pepper are . . .

[aláti]
and [pipéri]
stand for
salt and
pepper!

5. [áspro] άσπρο white

6. [mávro] μαύρο black

. . . the sea and sky are . . .

[thálasa] is sea
and [uranós]
is sky in Greek!

7. [ble]
   μπλε navy blue

8. [ghalázio]
   γαλάζιο sky blue

. . . coffee in a cafe? . . .

[kafés]
is the coffee
we drink!
and [kafé]
the colour.

9. [kafé] καφέ brown

The words for colors are important
for things we like or things we own.
For example "white is my favorite color"
or "I have a red Ferrari"! Look up in a
dictionary other colors not mentioned
here and write them down. By the way
[hróma] χρώμα is the word for "color"
in Greek.

Any connection
with the word
"chromatic" ?

43

10 The numbers one to ten (1-10) for you!

For more numbers you can also see Unit 12

Knowing how to say a few numbers in Greek will be useful on many different occasions while in Greece. For example, asking for a room number, buying a pack of cigarettes, giving out a telephone number, or even disclosing your age! Of course, if everything else fails, you can always count with your fingers in order to get one tomato instead of two but be aware that *finger counting* is not as universal as it appears to be. Below you can check the numbers 1 - 10 and the corresponding Greek finger counting!

The numbers 1-10

[éna]	[dhío]	[tría]
ένα	δύο	τρία
one	two	three

[tésera]
τέσσερα
four

 [pénde]
πέντε
five

You might also hear a slightly different version for "one" [énas] or [mía], "three" [tris], and "four" [téseris]. Notice that Greeks start counting with the index finger, making the thumb as number five instead of no. 1.

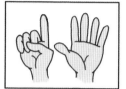 [éxi]
έξι
six

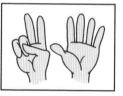 [eptá]
επτά
seven

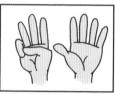 [októ]
οκτώ
eight

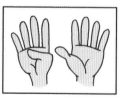 [eniá]
εννιά
nine

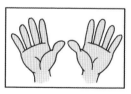 [dhéka]
δέκα
ten

Am I an actress yet?
    Eleven grimaces and
gestures to mimic...
            if you can!

!

Non-verbal communication, i.e. body language including gestures and grimaces, is as important to recognize as it is with the written or spoken word. The signs and messages conveyed through non-verbal language are often more important than the verbal language. You should only mimic the illustrations below if you are really sure and confident about the appropriate context for these grimaces and gestures.

Non - verbal "yes + no!"

"Yes" is [ne] ναι and "no" is [óchi] óxi in Greek!

1. The head moves forward with or without the word [no].

[ts]! No!

2. The head moves backwards, the eyebrowss are raised accompanied by a [ts] tongue clicking sound!

③
3. [no sound]
No idea!

④
4. [ti]?
What?

⑤
5. [na]!
Piss off!

⑥
6. [éla]! Come!
The palm moves
inwards.

7. [fíghe] Go away!
The palm is
moving outwards.

⑧
8. [faí]
Food!

9. [sound of a kiss]!
Excellent!

⑩
10. [grrr]!
I'm angry!

11. [trelós íse]?
Are you crazy?
The palm moves in
a circular motion

⑪

[ti óra íne]?
What time is it?

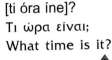

[ti óra íne]?
Τι ώρα είναι;
What time is it?

[íne] ...
Είναι...
It's ...

[mía]	[dhío]	[tris]	[téseris]
μία	δύο	τρεις	τέσσερις

[pénde]	[éxi]	[eptá]	[októ]
πέντε	έξι	επτά	οκτώ

[eniá]	[dhéka]	[éndeka]	[dhódheka]
εννιά	δέκα	έντεκα	δώδεκα

Units 8 & 10
can be
useful here!

[dhódheka to mesiméri]
Δώδεκα το μεσημέρι
Twelve o'clock noon.

[dhódheka ta mesánihta]
Δώδεκα τα μεσάνυχτα.
Twelve o'clock midnight.

Time is important when you want
to know opening and closing times
for instance:

[ti óra aníghi/klíni...]?
Τι ώρα ανοίγει/κλείνει...;
What time does... open/close?

to proinó?]
το πρωινό?
breakfast?

[ti óra íne...
Τι ώρα είναι...
What time is...

to mesimerianó?]
το μεσημεριανό?
lunch?

to vradhinó?]
βραδινό?
dinner?

1:55 δύο παρά πέντε
[dhío pará
pénde]
μία 1:00
[mía]
μία και πέντε 1:05
[mía ke
pénde]

1:50 δύο παρά δέκα
[dhío pará
dhéka]
μία και δέκα 1:10
[mía ke
dhéka]

1:45 δύο παρά τέταρτο
[dhío pará
tetarto]
μία και τέταρτο 1:15
[mía ke
tétarto]

1:40 δύο παρά είκοσι
[dhío pará
ikosi]
μία και είκοσι 1:20
[mía ke
íkosi]

1:35 δύο παρά είκοσι πέντε
[dhío pará
ikosipénde]
μία και είκοσι πέντε 1:25
[mía ke
ikosipénde

μία και μισή 1:30
[mía ke misi]

You should note that the hour comes before
the minutes when you use the words [ke]
past or [pará] to, e.g. [mía ke pénde] which
literally means "one (o'clock) past five
(minutes)! In contrast, the hour comes after
the minutes when you use the words [metá]
after or [prin] before, e.g. [pénde leptá metá
tis mía] five minutes after one.

B | The Essential Kit

The next twelve units can be used when meeting Greeks on several everyday occasions including hotel accommodations, drinking, eating, and shopping!

13 *Thirteen*! Are you superstitious about Greek? Important linking and key words.

14 The *fourteen* most frequent, everyday Greek verbs.

15 The *fifteen* most frequent, everyday expressions with "I am... " and "I want to... "!

16 Accommodation 1: Breaking the ice in hotels, pensions, youth hostels, and guest rooms.

17 Accommodation 2: What you might often hear or want to ask when looking for a room.

18 Breakfast... in Greece. Snacks and real Greek coffee.

19 Lunch in an ouzeri and dinner in a fish tavern or souvlaki eatery!

20 Appetizers, main courses, and desserts in Greece.

21 Sitting in a [zaharoplastío], [kafetéria], or [bar] for a coffee, sweets, or a glass of wine.

22 Grocery shopping in mini markets or vegetable street markets.

23 "An apple a day keeps the doctor away!" tasting a variety of Greek fruit.

24 The Greek alphabet: *twenty four* letters to decipher or what? Short - cuts for the worriers...

Thirteen! Are you superstitious about Greek? Important linking and key words.

In your early attempts to say something in Greek, the following list of linking and key words will be helpful especially if you try to learn it by heart. Of course, you don't have to and you can come back to this unit as often as needed.

yes	[ne]	ναι
no	[óchi]	όχι
and	[ke]	και
with	[me]	με
without	[horís]	χωρίς
or	[i]	ή

The letters k - l - m - n can create many words in Greek: [ke] - [me] - [ne] are already on the list above! If you add the sound [o] your list can expand: [kéo] I burn, [léo] I say, [néo] new! It's good to have fun with some word games, isn't it? Learning by associations is of immense value and boosts memory retention greatly. For example, "bite - kite - lite - site" can illustrate this in English by replacing the first letter with other possibilities!

Another trick you can use to expand vocabulary is to learn some linking words:

yes or no?	[ne] [i] [óhi]?	ναι ή όχι;
with...or...?	[me]... [i]...?	με... ή... ;
both...and...	[ke]... [ke]...	και... και...
either...or...	[i]... [i]...	ή... ή...

The following question-words will come in handy when constructing simple phrases:

*Question words
The "wh-words"
and "how"
question.*

what?	[ti]	τι;
when?	[póte]	πότε;
where?	[pu]	πού;
who?	[p-yós]	ποιος;
why?	[yatí]	γιατί;

how far?	[póso makriá]	πόσο μακριά;
how long?	[póso meghálo]	πόσο μεγάλο;
how much?	[póso polí]	πόσο πολύ;
how many?	[pósa polá]	πόσα πολλά;
how?	[pos]	πώς;

First of all, you don't need to know the alphabet to say or understand some Greek. Second of all, we have chosen only the absolutely essential and manageable chunks. So keep flipping your fingers over the pages back and forth without worrying about the details!

Still superstitious? Learn the Greek alphabet then on page 116.

The fourteen most frequent Greek verbs

Before we provide you with the list of the most frequently used verbs, we would like to draw your attention to the two most frequently used verbs not only in Greek but also in many other languages including English: the verbs "to be" and "to have".

The verb "to be" in Greek:

I am	[íme]	είμαι
you are	[íse]	είσαι
s/he/it is	[íne]	είναι
we are	[ímaste]	είμαστε
you are	[ísaste]	είσαστε
they are	[íne]	είναι

The verb "to have" in Greek:

I have	[ého]	έχω
you have	[échis]	έχεις
s/he/it has	[échi]	έχει
we have	[éhume]	έχουμε
you have	[éhete]	έχετε
they have	[éhun]	έχουν

The verbs no. 4, 6, 7, 9, 11,13,14 on the next page have the same endings as the verb "to have".

Notice that the personal pronouns, words like "I, you, they" are not necessarily needed in Greek, since the verb ending changes for each person.

Of course, they can be used with the verb just to emphasize the person involved in an action. These words are:

I [eghó] εγώ, you [esí] εσύ,
he [aftós] αυτός, she [aftí] αυτή,
it [aftó] αυτό, we [emís] εμείς,
you [esís] εσείς, they [aftí] αυτοί.

Personal pronouns: words like "I - you - we".

The sound and not the spelling of [aftí] stands for both "she" and "they". Equally, the sound of [íne] was for "he is", "she is", "it is", and "they are"! Yes, they all sound the same, but they are not difficult to be distinguished in context.

To, too, or two? They all sound the same!

The 14 most frequent verbs are:

1. ask	[rotáo]	ρωτάω
2. be hungry	[pináo]	πεινάω
3. be thirsty	[dhipsáo]	διψάω
4. buy	[aghorázo]	αγοράζω
5. come	[érhome]	έρχομαι
6. do/make	[káno]	κάνω
7. find	[vrísko]	βρίσκω
8. go	[páo]	πάω
9. know	[xéro]	ξέρω
10. like	[marési]	μ' αρέσει
11. see	[vlépo]	βλέπω
12. speak	[miláo]	μιλάω
13. think	[nomízo]	νομιζω
14. work	[dhulévo]	δουλεύω

You can read some rules about greek verbs on page 119.

15

The fifteen most frequent everyday expressions with "I am..." and "I want to..."!

You can definitely try to build simple phrases without any advanced knowledge of Greek. Below you can make use of phrases with "I am" and "I want to... "

I am...!

I am...   [íme]...   Είμαι...

...angry	...drunk	...happy
[thimoménos]	[methizménos]	[harúmenos]
θυμωμένος	μεθυσμένος	χαρούμενος

...in love	...sick‛	...tired
[erotevménos]	[árostos]	[kurazménos]
ερωτευμένος	άρρωστος	κουρασμένος

The ending -os is for men! If you are a woman you are supposed to change the ending of all six words above to -i! For example, [árostos] becomes [árosti] for a sick woman!

Here you can also learn the phrases "I'm okay!" or "I'm not okay!" as replies to the frequent question

"How are you?" [ti kánete] Τι κάνετε;

I'm okay!
[íme kalá]!
Είμαι καλά!

I'm not okay!
[íme áshima]
Είμαι άσχημα!

How are you?
I'm okay!
or I'm not okay!

I want to... [thélo na]... Θέλω να...

I want to...

...dance
[horépso]
χορέψω

...drink
[p-yo]
πιω

...eat
[fáo]
φάω

...leave
[fígho]
φύγω

...sing
[traghudhíso]
τραγουδήσω

...sleep
[kimithó]
κοιμηθώ

You can also substitute the phrase "I want to" with two other alternatives: "I have to... " [prépi na...] πρέπει να or "I may... " [borí na...] μπορεί να...

I have to go to the toilet!
[prépi na páo stin tualéta]!
Πρέπει να πάω στην τουαλέτα!

I have to...
I may...

See also Unit 14.

16

Accommodation 1: breaking the ice in hotels, pensions, youth hostels, and guest rooms.

Most places will have someone who speaks English to a certain degree. Below is much of what you need at odd times!

At the reception desk [reseptión] ρεσεψιόν

Good day, I would like a single room for one night.
[kaliméra, tha íthela éna monóklino ya mía níhta]
Καλημέρα, θα ήθελα ένα μονόκλινο για μία νύχτα.

We have a double room for 50 euro.
[éhume éna dhíklino ya penínda evró]
Έχουμε ένα δίκλινο για 50 ευρώ.

That's fine. Can I pay by credit card?
[endáxi. Boró na pliróso me pistotikí kárta]?
Εντάξει. Μπορώ να πληρώσω με πιστωτική κάρτα?

Of course.
[fisiká]
Φυσικά.

Can I look at the room?
[boró na dho to dhomátio]?
Μπορώ να δω το δωμάτιο?

No problem.
[kanéna próvlima]
Κανένα πρόβλημα.

Good, I will take it.
[oréa tha to páro]
Ωραία θα το πάρω.

The room number is 21 on the second floor.
[o arithmós dhomatíu íne ikosiéna ston dhéftero órofo]
Ο αριθμός δωματίου είναι 21 στον δεύτερο όροφο.

[!]

Watch out for:

ΞΕΝΟΔΟΧΕΙΟ
[xenodhohío]
HOTEL

ΞΕΝΩΝΑΣ
[xenónas]
YOUTH HOSTEL

ΠΑΝΣΙΟΝ
[pansión]
PENSION

ΔΩΜΑΤΙΑ
[dhomátia]
ROOMS ...to let

Below is an important vocabulary list that may come in handy on many different occasions. In case you want to complain about something if "it's not working properly" you can say [dhen dhulévi...] δεν δουλεύει or [hálase...] χάλασε... when it's "out of order"!

1. television	[i tileórasi]	η τηλεόραση
2. table	[to trapézi]	το τραπέζι
3. balcony door	[i balkonóporta]	η μπαλκονόπορτα
4. balcony	[to balkóni]	το μπαλκόνι
5. vase	[to vázo]	το βάζο
6. carpet	[to halí]	το χαλί
7. lamp	[i lámba]	η λάμπα
8. mirror	[o kathréftis]	ο καθρέφτης
9. towel	[i petséta]	η πετσέτα
10. shaving brush	[i vúrtsa xirízmatos]	η βούρτσα ξυρίσματος
11. toothbrush	[i odhondóvurtsa]	η οδοντόβουρτσα
12. razor	[to xiráfi]	το ξυράφι
13. washbasin	[o niptíras]	ο νιπτήρας
14. bed	[to kreváti]	το κρεβάτι
15. bed linen	[i kuvérta]	η κουβέρτα
16. painting	[o pínakas]	ο πίνακας
17. pillow	[to maxilári]	το μαξιλάρι
18. radio	[to rádhio]	το ράδιο
19. chair	[i karékla]	η καρέκλα
20. ventilator	[o anemistíras]	ο ανεμιστήρας
21. phone	[to tiléfono]	το τηλέφωνο
22. bedside cabinet	[to komodhíno]	το κομοδίνο

Out of order

Use [hálase] or [dhen dhoulévi] with some words from this list.

Accommodation 2: what you might hear often or want to ask when looking for a room.

It is definitely wise to have made reservations at home. If not, you might often hear or would like to ask some of the following phrases:

Grand Hotel, room reservations.
Can I help you?
[grand otél kratísis parakaló]
Γκραντ Οτέλ, κρατήσεις, παρακαλώ!

I would like to have
a room for tonight.
[tha íthela éna dhomátio ya apópse]
Θα ήθελα ένα δωμάτιο για απόψε.

Sorry, but we're full for tonight.
[sighnómi alá ímaste ghomáti símera]
Συγνώμη αλλά είμαστε
γεμάτοι σήμερα!

Do you have any rooms
for tomorrow?
[éhete kanéna dhomatio ya ávrio]?
Έχετε κανένα δωμάτιο για αύριο;

!

Have you made a reservation?
[éhete káni krátisi]?
Έχετε κάνει κράτηση;

How many days will you stay?
[póses méres tha mínete]?
Πόσες μέρες θα μείνετε;

What's your name please?
[t' ónoma sas parakaló]?
Τ' όνομά σας παρακαλώ;

May I see your passport?
[boró na dho to dhiavatírió sas]?
Μπορώ να δω το διαβατήριό σας;

Please, sign here!
[ipoghrápste edhó parakaló]
Υπογράψτε εδώ παρακαλώ!

Do you have a room...?
[éhete dhomátio]? Έχετε δωμάτιο... ;

You might
want to ask!

...with a view? [me théa]? με θέα;
...with a balcony? [me balkóni]? με μπαλκόνι;
...with a bath? [me bánio]? με μπάνιο;
...with a shower? [me duz]? με ντους;
...with a TV? [me tileórasi]? με τηλεόραση;
...with A/C? [me erkondísion]? με A/C;

Do you have a... room?
[éhete éna... dhomátio]? Έχετε ένα... δωμάτιο;
...bigger [meghalítero] μεγαλύτερο
...smaller [mikrótero] μικρότερο
...cheaper [pio ftinó] πιο φτηνό
...quieter [pio ísiho] πιο ήσυχο
...newer [pio kenúrio] πιο καινούριο

Is there a... ? [ipárhi...]? Υπάρχει... ;
...lift / elevator? [asansér]? ασανσέρ;
...bar? [bar]? μπαρ;
...cafe? [kafetéria]? καφετέρια;
...restaurant? [estiatório]? εστιατόριο;
...hairdresser? [komotírio]? κομμωτήριο;

In a larger hotel you might hear many English words used in Greek. Some are: manager [mánatzer] μάνατζερ, reception desk [reseptión] ρεσεψιόν (from French), bar [bar] μπαρ, mini bar [míni bar] μίνι μπαρ, lobby [lóbi] λόμπυ, suite [suíta] σουίτα, or service [sérvis] σέρβις.

Breakfast... in Greece. Snacks and real Greek coffee!

Most hotels offer breakfast in the morning. Continental or English breakfast is usually available in most places and a buffet breakfast sometimes. If breakfast is not available in the place you' re staying, you can always try to find a coffee house or a sandwich place. There apart from a coffee, tea or glass of milk you can also ask for a croissant [it is pronounced as that], a sesame bread [kulúri], or a sandwich [sándwits]. In the morning, you can always try a [tirópita] τυρόπιτα which is a cheese pie, a [spanakópita] σπανακόπιτα which is a spinach pie, or even a [bughátsa] μπουγάτσα which is an egg-custured pie. No matter what, be adventurous and try new tastes with peculiar names.

[tirópita]?
What is that?

bread	[psomí]	ψωμί
butter	[vútiro]	βούτυρο
cheese	[tirí]	τυρί
ham	[zambón]	ζαμπόν
honey	[méli]	μέλι
jam	[marmeládha]	μαρμελάδα
sugar	[záhari]	ζάχαρη
yogurt	[yaúrti]	γιαούρτι

Breakfast
in Greece!

coffee [kafé] καφέ   milk [ghála] γάλα   tea [tsái]

orange juice [himó portokáli]   cocoa [kakáo] κακάο
χυμό πορτοκάλι

To ask for one, say [éna... parakaló]
"a... please"! Most coffees are available
in Greece. You'll have the opportunity
to ask for a Greek coffee served in
a small espresso cup without sugar
[éna skéto parakaló!], with a spoon of
sugar [éna métrio parakaló!], or with two
spoons of sugar [éna ghlikó parakaló!].

cappuccino	[kaputsíno]	καπουτσίνο
espresso	[espréso]	εσπρέσσο
nes coffee	[nes kafé]	νες καφέ
iced coffee	[frapé]	φραπέ

with	[me]	με
without	[horís]	χωρίς
with milk	[me ghála]	με γάλα
without sugar	[horís záhari]	χωρίς ζάχαρη

egg/eggs	[avghó - avghá]	αυγό - αυγά
bacon and eggs	[béikon ke avghá]	μπέικον και αυγά
fried egg	[tighanitó]	τηγανιτό
ham and eggs	[zambón me avghá]	ζαμπόν με αυγά
hard boiled egg	[sfihtó]	σφιχτό
omelet	[omeléta]	ομελέτα
scrambled eggs	[anakateména]	ανακατεμένα
soft - boiled egg	[meláto]	μελάτο
sunny side - up	[máti]	μάτι

19 Lunch in an ouzeri and dinner in a fish tavern or souvlaki eatery!

Many Greeks have lunch as their main meal of the day. Of course, many have dinner as a second main meal eating quite late for northern European standards many times around 10 or 11 o'clock in the evening! Greeks usually eat lunch at home and dinner, which is an informal affair by the way, in a tavern. Many names are used in Greece for the eating places. Below is a guide to decipher most of them:

Obviously, visiting these places and having people willing to show you around the kitchen will enchance your under-standing!

ΕΣΤΙΑΤΟΡΙΟ [estiatório] restaurant
ΜΑΓΕΙΡΕΙΟΝ [maghiríon] restaurant with daily Greek stewed and oven specialties
ΜΕΖΕΔΟΠΩΛΕΙΟ [mezedhopolío] ouzeri eatery serving ouzo with assorted appetizer platters
ΟΥΖΕΡΙ [uzerí] ouzeri
ΠΙΤΣΕΡΙΑ [pitsería] pizzeria
ΣΟΥΒΛΑΤΖΙΔΙΚΟ [suvlatzídhiko] souvlakeri eatery serving souvlaki, ghiros, kalamaki
ΤΑΒΕΡΝΑ [tavérna] a less formal restaurant
ΧΑΣΑΠΟΤΑΒΕΡΝΑ [hasapotavérna] tavern specialized in assorted meat specialties
ΨΑΡΟΤΑΒΕΡΝΑ [psarotavérna] tavern serving many different fish dishes
ΨΗΣΤΑΡΙΑ [psistariá] tavern, a combination of souvlakeri and hasapotaverna with assorted meat dishes

Below is a list of important phrases to help you out when you want to ask for some things in a Greek place to eat:

How to ask for things in Greek!

- the menu / bill (check) please!
  [ton katálogho / loghariazmó parakaló]!
  Τον κατάλογο / λογαριασμό παρακαλώ!

- Can you give / bring me / us... ?
  [mu / mas dhínete / férnete...] ?
  Μου / μας δίνετε / φέρνετε... ;

- I like / I'd like... the today's special!
  [thélo / tha íthela... to piáto tis iméras]!
  Θέλω / θα ήθελα... το πιάτο της ημέρας.

- What would you recommend?
  [ti tha protínate]? Τι θα προτείνατε;

1. bottle of wine	[bukáli krasí]	μπουκάλι κρασί
2. chair	[karékla]	καρέκλα
3. salad	[saláta]	σαλάτα
4. wine glass	[potíri krasiú]	ποτήρι κρασιού
5. sauce bowl	[bol ya sáltsa]	μπολ για σάλτσα
6. plate	[piáto]	πιάτο
7. napkin	[petséta]	πετσέτα
8. candle	[kerí]	κερί
9. fork	[pirúni]	πιρούνι
10. knife	[mahéri]	μαχαίρι
11. bowl	[bol]	μπολ
12. platter	[piatéla]	πιατέλα
13. table cloth	[trapezomándilo]	τραπεζομάντιλο
14. table	[trapézi]	τραπέζι

At the table:
To ask for some things from this list, say [éna... parakaló]!
For items 1, 4, 5,6, 8, 9, 10, 11, 13 and 14.
The remaining items should be asked with [mía... parakaló]!

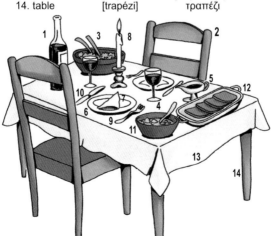

Check also Unit 17 or 19!

20 Appetizers, main courses, and desserts in Greece.

Food is obviously not for us to describe but for you to sample and taste! Traditional Greek cuisine is rich in delicacies and specialties are influenced by its local products especially olive oil and its neighbors around the Mediterranean Sea. Ask for local dishes in the places you visit since you can always find something that is not readily available all over Greece. There's a perfect way to try a little bit of everything in Greece and that's [pikilía] ποικιλία! It comes in small or large dishes, [mikrí pikilía] μικρή ποικιλία or [megháli pikilía] μεγάλη ποικιλία including small portions of many different appetizers for you to taste and judge! Most restaurant menus are written in both Greek and English. Sometimes the translation needs to be "deciphered" but somehow you can guide yourself through. Below, you find the main sections in a Greek menu and... good luck!

ΟΡΕΚΤΙΚΑ	[orektiká]	appetizers
ΜΕΖΕΔΕΣ	[mezédhes]	starters
ΣΑΛΑΤΕΣ	[salátes]	salads
ΛΑΔΕΡΑ	[ladherá]	cooked in oil
ΨΑΡΙΑ	[psária]	fish dishes
ΨΗΤΑ	[psitá]	grilled foods
ΜΑΓΕΙΡΕΥΤΑ	[maghireftá]	oven specialties
ΤΗΣ ΩΡΑΣ	[tis óras]	a la minute
ΕΠΙΔΟΡΠΙΑ	[epidhórpia]	desserts
ΓΛΥΚΑ	[ghliká]	tartes, sweets
ΠΟΤΑ	[potá]	beverages

While visiting or staying in Greece for some time we'd like to recommend some Greek specialties for you to taste:

- ΝΤΟΛΜΑΔΕΣ ΓΙΑΛΑΝΤΖΗ [dolmádhes yalantzí] grape leaves stuffed with rice.
- ΚΟΛΟΚΥΘΑΚΙΑ ΤΗΓΑΝΙΤΑ [kolokithákia tighanitá] fried zucchini.
- ΤΖΑΤΖΙΚΙ [tzatzíki] a yogurt dip with cucumber, garlic and oil.
- ΧΩΡΙΑΤΙΚΗ ΣΑΛΑΤΑ [horiátiki saláta] a salad made of tomatoes, cucumber, olives, onions, green peppers and feta cheese.

What appetizers?

- ΑΡΝΑΚΙ ΕΞΟΧΙΚΟ [arnáki exohikó] spiced baby lamb baked in a wax paper.
- ΓΙΟΥΒΕΤΣΙ [yiuvétsi] meat with orzo pasta.
- ΜΟΥΣΑΚΑΣ [musakás] layers of sliced eggplant and minced meat, oven - browned with bechamel sauce.
- ΝΤΟΜΑΤΕΣ ΓΕΜΙΣΤΕΣ [domátes ghemistés] tomatoes stuffed with rice.

What main course?

- ΓΑΛΑΚΤΟΜΠΟΥΡΕΚΟ [ghalaktobúreko] flaky pastry filled with custard, steeped in syrup.
- ΚΑΤΑΪΦΙ [kataífi] shredded pastry roll filled with walnuts and steeped in syrup.
- ΜΠΑΚΛΑΒΑΣ [baklavás] flaky pastry with a nut filling.

What dessert?

bartender [bárman] μπάρμαν
bottle [bukáli] μπουκάλι
buffet [bufés] μπουφές
chair [karékla] καρέκλα
counter [pángos] πάγκος
customer [pelátis] πελάτης
glass [potíri] ποτήρι
ice cream [paghotó] παγωτό
menu [katáloghos] κατάλογος
plate [piáto] πιάτο
table [trapézi] τραπέζι
toilet restroom [tualéta] τουαλέτα
utensils [maheropíruna] μαχαιροπίρουνα
waitress [servitóra] σερβιτόρα
wall - hanger [kremástra] κρεμάστρα

Sitting in a [zaharoplastío], [kafetéria] or [bar] for a coffee, sweets, or a glass of wine.

Also check Unit 18 or 20.

Many sunsets are spectacular in Greece. Especially if you are in a place with panoramic views of the sea's horizon or a mountain range. Many drinking and eating places have been built for that purpose on cliffs, shores and any other strategic location for "offering" the best view! There you can enjoy a coffee or a drink the "Greek way" which simply means that you sit comfortably, watch the surroundings leisurely and let the time go by! Watch out for the following signs before you make your next stop:

ΖΑΧΑΡΟΠΛΑΣΤΕΙΟ [zaharoplastío]
a coffee place having a selection of pastries, tarts, sweets and ice creams.

ΚΑΦΕΝΕΙΟ [kafenío] a coffee place usually used as a meeting point for locals who frequent there to have a Greek coffee, perhaps play cards or talk politics.

ΚΑΦΕΤΕΡΙΑ [kafetéria] this is not a cafeteria in a strict sense; it is rather a coffee place frequented mostly by younger crowds.

ΜΠΑΡ [bar] a morning bar can be a stop for a coffee or drink; an evening bar is usually for alcoholic beverages.

ΣΝΑΚ ΜΠΑΡ [snak bar] a snack bar serving sandwiches and other snacks along with coffee and most beverages.

Of course, you might experience some places with their own "flavor", "ambiance" and special "offers". Good luck!

Excuse me! [sighnómi]! Συγνώμn!
or [parakaló]! Παρακαλώ! are two phrases mostly used to get the attention of a waiter or waitress.
Some Greeks might clap their hands, snap their fingers, or even shout [pedhí]! παιδί! literally meaning "child!", but these methods are not recommended!

Note below:

Excuse me! [sighnómi] Συγνώμn!
Yes sir? [málista, kírie] Μάλιστα κύριε!

Yes madam? [málista kiría] Μάλιστα κυρία!

Can I please have the menu? [ton katálogho parakaló]! Τον κατάλογο παρακαλώ!

Right away! I'll be there. [amésos]! [éftasa]! Αμέσως! Έφτασα!

Thanks a lot! [efharistó polí]! Ευχαριστώ πολύ!

What would you recommend?
[ti tha protínate]? Τι θα προτείνατε;

How to get the attention of a waiter!

[parakaló]! is an important word. According to context it can mean:
1. "please"
2. "You 're welcome!"
3. "Hello!" on the phone or
4. "What can I do for you?" in a store.
A very important word, don't you think?

22 Grocery shopping in mini markets or vegetable street markets.

There is little language exchange in a large supermarket. You can always ask [pu íne...]? Πού είναι; Where's...? or [échete...]? Έχετε...; Do you have ...? for something you are looking for. The rest is checking simply the shelves for products you like and trust. In mini markets or street markets, perhaps you have to ask or say a few more things. The list below will help:

Θα ήθελα... [tha íthela]... I'd like...

ένα κουτί... [éna kutí]... a pack/box of...

*I'd like...
a pack -
package -
box -
or piece of...*

τσιγάρα [tsighára] cigarettes
σπίρτα [spírta] matches
ασπιρίνες [aspirínes] aspirins

ένα πακέτο... [éna pakéto]... a packet of...

βούτυρο [vútiro] butter
χαλβά [halvá] halva
μακαρόνια [makarónia] spaghetti

ένα κομμάτι... [éna komáti]... a piece of...

ψωμί [psomí] bread
τυρί [tirí] cheese
κρέας [kréas] meat

In most Greek towns you'll come across a vegetable and flower street market: ΛΑΪΚΗ ΑΓΟΡΑ [laikí aghorá]! It's an interesting experience to mingle among street vendors and people pushing or pulling shopping carts all different directions at once! Point out and taste some of the following vegetables. Most of them are sold by the kilo: [éna kiló] ένα κιλό one kilo or [dhío kilá] δύο κιλά two kilos will do the trick for the quantities you want.

Greek vegetables are good!

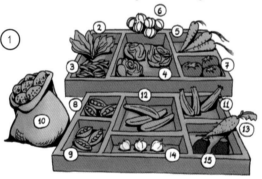

1. vegetables	[lahaniká]	λαχανικά
2. lettuces	[marúlia]	μαρούλια
3. fresh beans	[fasolákia]	φασολάκια
4. cabbage	[láhana]	λάχανα
5. carrots	[karóta]	καρότα
6. garlic	[skórdho]	σκόρδο
7. tomatoes	[domátes]	ντομάτες
8. peas	[bizélia]	μπιζέλια
9. beans	[fasólia]	φασόλια
10. potatoes	[patátes]	πατάτες
11. zucchini	[kolokithákia]	κολοκυθάκια
12. cucumbers	[angúria]	αγγούρια
13. radish	[radhíkia]	ραδίκι
14. onions	[kremídhia]	κρεμμύδια
15. eggplants	[melitzánes]	μελιτζάνες

Check how many words sound the same in both languages (numbers 5, 7, 10...)

Read also Unit 23.

23 "An apple a day keeps the doctor away!"

(greek proverb)

Read also Unit 22

Tasting and eating many different fruit in Greece is highly recommended! The country produces many different kinds of fruit throughout the year starting with apples, grapes, or watermelons to bananas and even kiwis! Some important phrases are listed below:

-How much is it? How much are they?
[póso káni]? [póso kánun]?
Πόσο κάνει; Πόσο κάνουν;

-A little bit more / less please!
[lígho pio polí / lígho parakaló]!
Λίγο πιο πολύ / λίγο παρακαλώ!

-I'd like... Can you give me... Let me have...
[tha íthela]...[dhóste mu]...[válte mu]...
Θα ήθελα...Δώστε μου...Βάλτε μου...

-Anything else? Nothing else thanks!
[típota álo]? [típota álo efharistó]!
Τίποτα άλλο; Τίποτα άλλο, ευχαριστώ!

Cherries,
suberb cherries!
[kerásia]
[álfa-álfa kerásia]!
Κεράσια!
Άλφα - άλφα κεράσια!

They look nice!
[oréa fénonde]
Ωραία φαίνονται!

Would you like a taste?
[thélete na dhokimásete]?
Θέλετε να δοκιμάσετε;

Mmm, delicious!
Can you give me
a kilo?
[hm] [polí oréa]!
[dhóste mu éna kiló].
Χμ, πολύ ωραία!
Δώστε μου ένα κιλό.

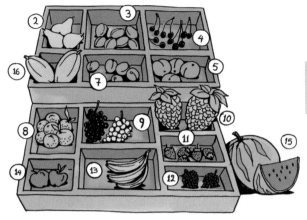

1. fruit	[frúta]	φρούτα
2. pears	[ahládhia]	αχλάδια
3. plums	[dhamáskina]	δαμάσκηνα
4. cherries	[kerásia]	κεράσια
5. peaches	[rodhákina]	ροδάκινα
6. nectarines	[nektarínia]	νεκταρίνια
7. apricots	[veríkoka]	βερίκοκα
8. oranges	[portokália]	πορτοκάλια
9. grapes	[stafília]	σταφύλια
10. pineapple	[ananás]	ανανάς
11. strawberries	[fráules]	φράουλες
12. blackberries	[vatómura]	βατόμουρα
13. bananas	[banánes]	μπανάνες
14. apples	[míla]	μήλα
15. watermelons	[karpúzia]	καρπούζια
16. yellow melons	[pepónia]	πεπόνια

Many street vendors like to select the fruits for you! Try to pick and choose yourself, otherwise if this is not possible, at least you can point and say: [aftó]! This one! or [aftá]! These ones!

The Greek alphabet: twenty-four letters to decipher or what? Shortcuts for worriers...

The Greek alphabet is so intimidating!

Read also pages 116-119

Many people who want to learn Greek express their fears about the alphabet. Do you really have to know the alphabet though in order to say a few things in Greek? We don't think so! And this book at hand was designed in such a way to cut some corners and break some rules to make your life easier and your experience more positive. Where knowing a few things about the alphabet becomes handy is when you read out some signs and try to orient yourself. Below we set out some shortcuts for you.

Shortcut 1!

You'll encounter many signs in English! A recent trend is that many stores will have their signs in English especially in tourist destinations. Many street signs are also bilingual especially on newly-paved roads or newly-opened freeways. The important signs of STOP or WC will appear as that!

Shortcut 2!

Do you really have to read the sign when walking by a Greek bakery? Probably not! You will smell

the aroma before you see the sign of
ΑΡΤΟΠΩΛΕΙΟΝ or ΑΡΤΟΠΟΙΕΙΟΝ. Similarly
it will not be necessary for you to read
ΚΡΕΟΠΩΛΕΙΟΝ when walking by
a butcher's. A goat on a hook, we
believe, will get your attention! We are
also sure that seeing the place and not
the sign ΠΡΑΤΗΡΙΟ ΒΕΝΖΙΝΗΣ petrol / gas
station will make the difference. Right?

The letters A, E, Z, K, M, N, O, T
present no difficulty as they look and
sound exactly like the corresponding
English letters. The letters B, H, P, I, Y, X,
need special attention as they resemble
English letters but represent quite
different sounds.

The remaining letters Γ, Δ, Θ, Λ, Ξ,
Π, Σ, Φ, Ψ, Ω are unique in the Greek
alphabet!

*Oops!
I've just missed
the gas station!*

Shortcut 3!

i. ΚΛΕΙΣΤΟΝ [klistón]
   CLOSED!

ii. ΕΚΤΟΣ ΛΕΙΤΟΥΡΓΙΑΣ!
   [ektós liturghías]
   OUT OF ORDER!

iii. ΑΠΑΓΟΡΕΥΕΤΑΙ ΤΟ
   ΠΑΡΚΙΝ / Η ΣΤΑΘΜΕΥΣΗ!
   [apaghorévete to párkin
   / i státhmefsi] No parking

iv. ΕΛΞΑΤΕ [élxate] PULL!

v. ΩΘΗΣΑΤΕ [othísate]
   PUSH!

vi. ΕΚΠΤΩΣΕΙΣ
   [ekptósis] SALES!

Important signs!

!

ΠΑΡΚΙΝ
*stands for
"car-park"*
ΣΤΑΘΜΕΥΣΗ
*is the Greek
word for
"parking".*

C   The necessary kit

The next twelve units can
be used when traveling
around Greece. Situations
include important phrases
and information about
methods of transport,
travel agencies, money
exchange, postal services,
camping, swimming,
and some unpleasant
emergencies.

25 The borders, customs, and papers.

26 Transportation 1: Take the train to the plane! (...trains).

27 Transportation 2: Take the train to the plane! (...planes).

28 Crossing the Mediterranean Sea in a sailing boat, cruise liner, or ferryboat.

29 Taking a Greek taxi. What an experience! I'd better take the bus or... walk!

30 Driving in Greece: Is it necessary to change your driving style?

31 Reading maps and asking for directions. Lost? So what?

32 The weather forecast: Another sunny day again tomorrow...

33 On the beach! Where? You've got 15,000 km of shoreline to choose from!

34 Hello! What's your name? Where are you from? How are you today?

35 Post office and bank: Two necessary stops while traveling.

36 Minor medical emergencies: Tips for everyday symptoms.

The border, customs and papers.

 There are numerous flights from many different countries to Greece. To include some: ΓΑΛΛΙΑ [ghalía] France, ΓΕΡΜΑΝΙΑ [ghermanía] Germany, ΑΓΓΛΙΑ [anglía] England, or ΑΜΕΡΙΚΗ [amerikí], USA. The following are the border crossings if you drive:

CHECK POINT	PREFECTURE	COUNTRY
ΚΗΠΟΙ [kípi]	ΕΒΡΟΥ [évru]	ΤΟΥΡΚΙΑ [turkía] Turkey
ΚΑΣΤΑΝΙΕΣ [kastaniés]	ΕΒΡΟΥ [évru]	ΤΟΥΡΚΙΑ [turkía] Turkey
ΠΡΟΜΑΧΩΝ [promahón]	ΣΕΡΡΩΝ [serón]	ΒΟΥΛΓΑΡΙΑ [vulgharía] Bulgaria
ΕΥΖΩΝΟΙ [évzoni]	ΚΙΛΚΙΣ [kilkís]	ΣΚΟΠΙΑ [skópia] FYROM
ΝΙΚΗ [níki]	ΦΛΩΡΙΝΑΣ [flórinas]	ΣΚΟΠΙΑ [skópia] FYROM
ΚΑΚΑΒΙΑ [kakaviá]	ΙΩΑΝΝΙΝΩΝ [ioanínon]	ΑΛΒΑΝΙΑ [alvanía] Albania

ΕΙΔΗ ΠΡΟΣ ΔΗΛΩΣΗ   ΤΙΠΟΤΑ ΓΙΑ ΔΗΛΩΣΗ

Goods to declare!   Nothing to declare!

Many tourists enter Greece by
boat from ΙΤΑΛΙΑ [italía] Italy through
ΚΕΡΚΥΡΑ [kérkira] Corfu, [pátra] Patras, or
ΑΘΗΝΑ [athína] Athens.
EU members can enter Greece with a
valid ID or passport. A valid passport is
required for any other country. At the
airports most signs are bilingual and we
hope you will always find airport staff
who can assist you in English. Some
important words and phrases:

ΑΦΙΞΕΙΣ

ΑΝΑΧΩΡΗΣΕΙΣ

ARRIVALS   DEPARTURES

bag, handbag	[tsánda]	τσάντα
car registration papers	[hartiá]	χαρτιά
citizenship	[ipikoótita]	υπηκοότητα
customs	[teloníon]	τελωνείον
driver's license	[ádhia odhíghisis]	άδεια οδήγησης
luggage	[aposkevés]	αποσκευές
nationality	[ethnikótita]	εθνικότητα
passport	[dhiavatírio]	διαβατήριο
suitcase	[valítsa]	βαλίτσα

· Your passport, please.
  [to dhiavatírio sas parakaló]
  Το διαβατήριό σας παρακαλώ.
· Open the luggage, please.
  [aníxte tis valítses parakaló]
  Ανοίξτε τις βαλίτσες παρακαλώ.
· Where are you coming from / going to?
  [apó pu érheste]? [pu páte]?
  Από πού έρχεστε; Πού πάτε;

Where are
you from?
[apó pu íste?]
Από πού είστε;

26 Transportation 1:
Take the train
to the plane! (...trains)

The new Athens Metro system, ΜΕΤΡΟ [metró] or ΗΛΕΚΤΡΙΚΟΣ [ilektrikós], added two new lines to the only one existing at the turn of the century. So Athenians can go now from Piraeus port ΛΙΜΑΝΙ ΠΕΙΡΑΙΩΣ [limáni pireós] to Kifisia and northern suburbs, to Peristeri and western suburbs, to Stavros and the newly built airport to the East, or to Ilioupoli and southern suburbs. Most destinations take half an hour to an hour to reach.

The Greek Interrail Organization, ΟΣΕ [osé], connects western Greece with Athens via the Peloponnese Railway Station, ΣΤΑΘΜΟΣ ΠΕΛΟΠΟΝΝΗΣΟΥ [stathmós peloponísu] and northern Greece via the Larisa Railway Station, ΣΤΑΘΜΟΣ ΛΑΡΙΣΗΣ [stathmós larísis].

**One way
or round trip?**

A ticket to
Piraeus please.
[éna isitírio
ya pireá parakaló]
Ένα εισιτήριο
για Πειραιά
παρακαλώ.

Single or return?
[apló i met'epistrofís]?
Απλό ή μετ'
επιστροφής;

Single, please.
[apló parakaló]
Απλό παρακαλώ.

When does the next train leave?
[póte févghi to epómeno tréno]?
Πότε φεύγει το επόμενο τρένο;

At 10:30 on platform 3.
[stis dhéka ke misí stin platfórma tría]
Στις δέκα και μισή στην πλατφόρμα τρία.

What time does it ... arrive / come by / leave?
[ti óra ... ftáni / pernái / févghi]?
Τι ώρα ... φτάνει / περνάει / φεύγει;

What time does it arrive / leave?

το τρένο
[to tréno]
the train

το πλοίο
[to plío]
the boat

το αεροπλάνο
[to aeropláno]
the plane

το λεωφορείο
[to leoforío]
the bus

arrival	[áfixi]	άφιξη
calling at	[antapókrisi]	ανταπόκριση
departure	[anahórisi]	αναχώρηση
express train	[tahía]	ταχεία
platform	[platfórma]	πλατφόρμα
railroad	[sidhiródhromos]	σιδηρόδρομος
station	[stathmós]	σταθμός
ticket	[isitírio]	εισιτήριο
timetable	[dhromolóya]	δρομολόγια
track	[ghramí]	γραμμή
train	[tréno]	τρένο

Highlight the words which have similar sounds in both languages! Perhaps express, station, train?

Transportation 2: Take the train to the plane! (...planes)

The new *Athens airport* "Eleftherios Venizelos" was built in 2001 and replaced "Ellinikon". It is a modern, international airport with the majority of the signs in both Greek and English.

In the last ten years or so, many other smaller airports on the mainland and some islands have become international airports having direct charter flights from many countries including ΣΟΥΗΔΙΑ [suidhía] Sweden, ΔΑΝΙΑ [dhanía] Denmark, and ΓΕΡΜΑΝΙΑ [ghermanía] Germany. The monopoly of ΟΛΥΜΠΙΑΚΗ ΑΕΡΟΠΟΡΙΑ [olimbiakí aeroporía] Olympic Airways does not longer exist; now one can take a domestic flight with many private companies including ΚΡΟΝΟΣ [krónos] Cronos, Air Greece, or Air Manos among others.

All domestic flights are non-smoking flights at the present. Some important phrases at an airport setting include:

- I'd like to change / cancel my flight.
  [tha íthela n' aláxo / n' akiróso tin ptísi mu]
  Θα ήθελα ν'αλλάξω / ν'ακυρώσω την πτήση μου.
- When do I have to be at the airport?
  [póte prépi na íme sto aerodhrómio]?
  Πότε πρέπει να είμαι στο αεροδρόμιο;

- Is it leaving on time? Is there a delay?
  [févghi stin óra tu]? [échi kathistérisi]?
  Φεύγει στην ώρα του; Έχει καθυστέρηση;
- Excuse me where is Exit No. 10?
  [sighnómi pu íne i éxodhos arithmós 10]?
  Συγνώμη, πού είναι η έξοδος αριθμός 10;

-A seat by the window / in the middle / at the aisle
[mía thési sto paráthiro / stin mési / ston dhiádhromo]
μία θέση στο παράθυρο / στη μέση / στον διάδρομο

-A business class / A class / economy class
[mia thési business / próti thési / ikonomikí thési]
μία θέση business / πρώτη θέση / οικονομική θέση

I would like to book
a flight to Rhodes.
[tha íthela na klíso
mia thési ya tin
ródho]
Θα ήθελα να κλείσω
μια θέση για τη Ρόδο.

For when?
[ya póte]?
Για πότε;

At the airport.
[sto aerodhrómio]
Στο αεροδρόμιο.

Tomorrow.
[ávrio]
Αύριο.

One way?
[apló]?
Απλό;

αεροδρόμιο
is literally
aerodrome
in English.
Airport is
[aeroliménas]
αερολιμένας *and*
[liménas] stands
for "port" alone.
Did you find
any other
similarities
in this unit?

Return trip.
[met'epistrofís]
Μετ' επιστροφής.

There is a flight
at 5:00 o'clock. OK?
[ipárhi mia ptísi stis
pénde i óra] [endáksi]?
Υπάρχει μια πτήση
στις 5:00 η ώρα.
Εντάξει;

At 5:00? Is there
anything earlier?
[stis pénde]? [ipárchi
káti pyo norís]?
Στις 5:00; Υπάρχει
κάτι πιο νωρίς;

I'm sorry, all other
flights are fully booked
[lipáme] [óles i áles
ptísis ine ghemátes]
Λυπάμαι όλες οι άλλες
πτήσεις είναι γεμάτες.

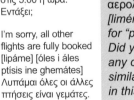

28 Crossing the Mediterranean Sea in a sailing boat, cruise liner, or ferryboat.

Water has always played an important role in Greek history. It is not accidental that Greek shipping is amongst the largest in the world, and for the size of the country it is, we believe this is a great achievement. Many people visit Greece in a sailing boat or take the very popular cruises with many island-hopping. Others get their experience by going from island to island or from the mainland to an island or vice - versa. The main harbor is in Piraeus where most destinations are served. Rafina port, one hour away from Athens, offers also certain connections to nearby islands. There are numerous travel agencies or internet sites to give you the most updated information regarding destinations and timetables. ΟΛΠ [olp] is the state - run organization responsible for the day - to - day business in Piraeus.

Boats, ships and yachts

boat	[várka]	βάρκα
cruise liner	[kruazieróplio]	κρουαζιερόπλοιο
ferryboat	[féribot]	φέρρυμποτ
fishing boat	[psaróvarka]	ψαρόβαρκα
motor boat	[mihanokínito]	μηχανοκίνητο
sailing boat	[istiofóro]	ιστιοφόρο

ship	[plío]	πλοίο
ship	[karávi]	καράβι
vessel	[skáfos]	σκάφος
yacht	[yot]	γιωτ

1. hold car park [ambári plíu] [hóros státhmefsis]
   αμπάρι πλοίου / χώρος στάθμευσης
2. deck [katástroma] κατάστρωμα
3. baggage - trolley [karotsáki] καροτσάκι
4. left - luggage office [hóros aposkevón]
   χώρος αποσκευών
5. emergency telephone [tiléfono anágis]
   τηλέφωνο ανάγκης
6. emergency exit [éxodhos kindhínu] έξοδος κινδύνου

All aboard!

1. At the harbor	[sto limáni]	Στο λιμάνι
2. pier	[apováthra]	αποβάθρα
3. ferryboat	[féribot]	φέρρυμπατ
4. trap - door	[bukapórta]	μπουκαπόρτα
5. gangway	[kinití skála]	κινητή σκάλα
6. Passport control	[élenhos dhiavatiríon]	έλεγχος διαβατηρίων
7. customs control	[teloniakós élenhos]	τελωνειακός έλεγχος

Taking a Greek taxi. What an experience! I'd better take the bus or... walk!

Some tips before you take a taxi!

Not all professional taxi drivers are the same. Unfortunately, this profession does not have a very high reputation or esteem in Greece. We hope that you don't have any unpleasant experience since many of them are knowledgeable and honest professionals. The few tips here will make you more aware about taking a taxi: 1) the taximeter should be on during the entire trip. 2) There is a daytime and a nighttime charge. The first is marked with the number 1 and the latter with the number 2 on the taximeter. Nighttime is more expensive and runs from 12:00 midnight to 6:00 a.m. 3) There is a price list by the taximeter of extra charges like suitcases, airport pick-ups, etc. 4) It is common in Athens to share the taxi with other passengers. 5) It is possible nowadays to make prior arrangements for a taxi to pick you up and take you to a certain destination. There are many taxi companies or taxi stands who operate by telephone appointments. 6) Taxis are easily detected by color and the taxi sign on the top. Taxis are yellow in Athens, but grey or blue taxis can be found in other cities and towns. The taxi sign reads TAXI in English or TAΞI [taxí] in Greek. 7) It is also possible to make reservations for a limousine

Look out for TAXI or TAΞI !

pick-up or an all-day excursion. 8) You can always hail a passing taxi. Many will slow down to hear the destination you're going, so if they do not come to a full stop you should... shout or at least speak loud!

- Is there a taxi - rank / stand around here?
  [ipárhi stathmós taxí edhó kondá]?
  Υπάρχει σταθμός ταξι εδώ κοντά;
- Please take me ... / take us ...
  [parakaló párte me ... / párte mas ...]
  Παρακαλώ πάρτε με .../ πάρτε μας ...]
- .. to the hotel ... to the city center...
  [sto xenodhohío ...] [sto kéndro tis pólis ...]
  ... στο ξενοδοχείο... στο κέντρο της πόλης...
- ... to the airport ... to the harbor ...
  [sto aerodhrómio...] [sto limáni...]...
  στο αεροδρόμιο... στο λιμάνι...
- to the bus terminal... to the train station ...
  [sto stathmó leoforíon ...] [sto stathmó trénon ...]
  στο σταθμό λεωφορείων... στο σταθμό τρένων...
- to this street / square / address ...
  [s'aftón ton dhrómo / s'aftín tin platía
  / s'aftín tin dhiéfthinsi ...]
  σ'αυτόν τον δρόμο / σ'αυτήν την πλατεία
  / σ'αυτήν την διεύθυνση...
- Please straight / left / right here!
  [parakaló ísia / aristerá / dhexiá edhó]
  Παρακαλώ ίσια / αριστερά / δεξιά εδώ!
- Please stop / turn here!
  [parakaló stamatíste / strípste edhó]
  Παρακαλώ σταματήστε / στρίψτε εδώ!
- How much do I owe you?
  [ti sas ofílo]? Τι σας οφείλω;
- I would like a receipt, please!
  [mia apódhixi parakaló]
  Μια απόδειξη παρακαλώ!
- This is for you!
  [aftó íne ya sas] Αυτό είναι για σας!

Important phrases to get you there!

5% to 10% can be added as a tip to the total taxi - fare!

30 Driving in Greece:
Is it necessary to change
your driving style?

*Tips for
the road!*

*Find out
beforehand
about
roadservice
companies!
ΕΛΠΑ [elpa]
is one of
the largest.*

In car-rental places almost everyone
speaks English and most major international
companies are represented in Greece.
You need a valid driver's license, a
passport or an EU police identification card,
and a major credit card before you hire a
car. Once on the road, we suggest that you
keep some tips in your mind: 1) Roads and
freeways are not always kept up or newly
paved. 2) Road signs might only be in
Greek. 3) Many, especially young,
drivers drive aggressively, by tailing too
close or not signaling when changing lanes
for instance. 4) Many street signs
including traffic lights are not observed fully
by everybody. 5) Several front-end
collision accidents in Greece are caused by
the absence of barriers between
dividing lanes. Not only the aforementioned
tips but also the unfamiliar destinations can
and should make you more aware and
cautious. With regard to your driving style,
use your best judgement! People usually say
that "the slower you drive, the faster you
get there"! It might be true for most of us,
right? On the overleaf you see a number of
situational words to help you when you're
on the road. *Be careful and drive safely!*

automatic car	[aftómato]	αυτόματο
car / automobile	[aftokínito]	αυτοκίνητο
catalytic car	[katalitikó]	καταλυτικό
shift car	[me tachítites]	με ταχύτητες

Do not lend your car and your...!

street	[odhós]	οδός
road	[dhrómos]	δρόμος
avenue	[leofóros]	λεωφόρος
motorway	[aftokinitó-	αυτοκινητό-
/highway	dhrómos]	δρομος
interstate	[ethnikí odhós]	εθνική οδός

On the road again...!

car shop	[sinerghío]	συνεργείο
gasoline/petrol	[venzíni]	βενζίνη
lights	[fóta]	φώτα
oil	[ládhi]	λάδι
petrol	[pratírio	πρατήριο
/gas station	venzínis]	βενζίνης
colloquially	[venzinádhiko]	βενζινάδικο
super	[súper]	σούπερ
tire	[ródha]	ρόδα
unleaded	[amólivdhi]	αμόλυβδη

At the petrol / gas station!

Check also Unit 31 about directions.

Some road signs :

1. No right turn
2. No U turn
3. Traffic merges
   from right
4. Customs
5. Toll station
6. Keep 70m
   distance
7. Stop
8. Ditch ahead
9. Uneven road

Reading maps and asking for directions. Lost? So what?

A phrase book, a dictionary and a map are perhaps three essential accessories when visiting a new place. Below and overleaf you find several possibilities to help you when you feel lost in a new place.

Where's the... ? [pu íne to...]? Πού είναι το...

...kiosk?
[períptero]?
περίπτερο;

... milk bar?
[ghalaktopolío]
γαλακτοπωλείο

grocery store?
[pandopolío]?
παντοπωλείο;

...butcher?
[kreopolío]
κρεοπωλείο

...baker?
[artopiíon]
αρτοποιείο

haberdasher?
[psilikatzídhiko]
ψιλικατζίδικο

*Look up
some other
possibilities
in the glossaries!*

...hotel?
[xenodhochío]
ξενοδοχείο;

...travel agency?
[praktorío]
πρακτορείο;

...restaurant?
[estiatório]
εστιατόριο;

All the places on the previous page were neuter nouns which simply means that they use the article το [to] in Greek corresponding to the English "the". Unfortunately, this is not always the case, so you might hear some variations if the noun is masculine or feminine! The glossaries at the back of this bookstate the gender of each noun you might want to use. Note the changes:

Check also some explanations on page 118.

| Where is the... station? [pu íne o stathmós]? Πού είναι ο σταθμός; | Where is the... bank? [pu íne i trápeza]? Πού είναι η τράπεza; | Where is the... cinema? [pu íne to sinemá]? Πού είναι το σινεμά; |

Directions are often not easy to give or follow. It becomes even harder when you are supposed to understand them in a breathless stream of Greek sounds and gestures! Be patient and ask again.

What? How did you say that? What first?

| Left! [aristerá] Αριστερά! | Straight [efthía] Ευθεία! | Right! [dhexiá] Δεξιά! |

You might also hear [páno] πάνω! or [káto]! κάτω! if there is an uphill or downhill, or [próto/dhéftero stenó] πρώτο/δεύτερο στενό for "first/second side-street". [bros] μπρος and [píso] πίσω stand for front/ahead and behind/back.

Check also Unit 4.

Many people talk about Greece with "the triple - s" motto: sun - sea - sand! Although Greece is pretty sunny throughout the year, it does have some rainy or snowy days. Especially, northern Greece can have temperatures below 0°C for couple (!) months in the middle of winter! So be prepared for... the worst, although we believe that you'll enjoy the Greek weather overall. The typical question is: What's the weather like? [ti keró káni/éhi]? Τι καιρό κάνει /έχει; Both verbs can be used here. Of course, don't use [káni] and [éhi] together!

What's the weather like?

It's drizzling.
[psihalízei]
Ψιχαλίζει.

It's raining.
[vréhi]
Βρέχει.

It's snowing.
[hionízi]
Χιονίζει.

It's sunny.
[éhi liakádha]
Έχει λιακάδα.

It's cloudy.
[éhi sinefiá]
Έχει συννεφιά.

It's windy.
[éhi aéra]
Έχει αέρα.

It's hot!
[káni zésti]!
Κάνει ζέστη!

It's cold!
[káni krío]
Κάνει κρύο!

climate	[klíma]	κλίμα
degrees	[vathmí]	βαθμοί
humidity	[ighrasía]	υγρασία
snow	[hióni]	χιόνι
sun	[ílios]	ήλιος
temperature	[thermokrasía]	θερμοκρασία
weather	[kerós]	καιρός
wind	[ánemos]	άνεμος

In Greek it doesn't rain "cats and dogs", it rains "chair legs"! The phrase is: "βρέχει καρεκλοπόδαρα!" [vréhi kareklopódhara]! Also "rain in sheets or buckets" can be rendered as "Βροχή με το τουλούμι!" [vrohí me to tulúmi]! in Greek...

Centigrade or Fahrenheit?

To convert centigrade into degrees Fahrenheit, multiply centigrade by 1.8 and add 32! No kidding! To convert degrees Fahrenheit into centigrade, subtract 32 from Fahrenheit and divide by 1.8! Do you need a calculator for that? You bet!

...with thunder and lightning
...[me vrondés ke astrapés]
...με βροντές και αστραπές

...variable!
...[ástatos]!
...άστατος!

Sometimes,
...not often
the weather is...
[o kerós íne...]
ο καιρός είναι...

33 On the beach! Where?
You 've got 15.000 km of
shore line to choose from!

There are 12,000,000 tourists visiting Greece on a yearly basis. Most of them come between late spring and early autumn although there is an increasing number of people who prefer cooler weather, so they visit Greece in the winter. Although world pollution has dramatically increased in recent years and the Mediterranean Sea has been affected by that, Greece is still proud to present some of the cleanest beaches in southern Europe. Many beaches have a flag nowadays designating that the beach has been kept clean. On some beaches you can rent a deck-chair and a beach umbrella. The GNTO (Greek National Tourist Organization) has much information and many brochures about almost all parts of Greece. Their offices are located all over Greece and they are a good stop before your explorations and adventures.

1. umbrella [ombréla] ομπρέλα
2. chair [karékla] καρέκλα
3. deck chair [xaplóstra] απλώστρα
4. canoe [kanó] κανώ
5. paddle boat [várka me petáli] βάρκα με πετάλι

1. bikini	[bikíni]	μπικίνι
2. sun cream	[kréma ilíu]	κρέμα ηλίου
3. sunglasses	[yaliá ilíu]	γυαλιά ηλίου
4. parasol	[ombréla]	ομπρέλα
5. hat	[kapélo]	καπέλο
6. bathing towel	[petséta]	πετσέτα
7. ball	[bála]	μπάλα
8. boat	[plío]	πλοίο
9. thermos can	[thermó]	θερμό
10. bucket	[kuvás]	κουβάς
11. camera	[fotoghrafikí mihaní]	φωτογραφική μηχανή
12. air mattress/lilo	[stróma]	στρώμα
13. flippers	[pédhila]	πέδιλα
14. shovel	[ftiári]	φτυάρι
15. rake	[tsugrána]	τσουγκράνα
16. book	[vivlío]	βιβλίο
17. net	[dhíhti]	δίχτυ
18. snorkel	[anapnefstíras]	αναπνευστήρας
19. goggles	[máska]	μάσκα
20. bathing suit	[mayó]	μαγιό
21. ice - cream	[paghotó]	παγωτό
22. cooler	[psighiáki]	ψυγειάκι
23. drinks	[potá]	ποτά

If you want to rent a parasol and a beach chair, you can ask [póso káni i ombréla ke i xaplóstra] πόσο κάνει η ομπρέλα και η ξαπλώστρα; People who rent on the beach are supposed to give you a receipt! Ask for it!

[mía apódhixi parakaló]
Μία απόδειξη παρακαλώ!
A receipt please!

95

Hello! What's your name?
Where are you from?
How are you today?

These are probably the most frequent questions Greeks like to ask. So be prepared to tell them a few things in Greek and surprise them. Greetings were presented in Units 1, 3, and 8. Skim through these units to refresh your memory about [yásu], [yásas] or even [kaliméra] and [kalispéra]!

Units 1, 3 and 8!

The typical question of asking somebody's name is [pos se léne]? or [pos sas léne]? Πώς σε / σας λένε; What's your name? Greek has many alternative ways of replying to this question.

My name is Maria!
[me léne maría]
Με λένε Μαρία!

My name is Helen!
[léghome eléni]
Λέγομαι Ελένη!

My name is Nick!
[onomázome níkos]
Ονομάζομαι Νίκος!

My name is Kostas!
[t' ónoma mu íne kóstas]
Τ΄όνομά μου είναι Κώστας!

Just the name would have also been fine!

Did you notice the different ways they give their names?

The typical question of finding out somebody's country is [apó pu íse]? or [apó pu íste]? Από πού είσαι / είστε; Where are you from? The typical reply is [íme apó...] Είμαι από... I'm from... Notice that an article is needed in Greek before the name of the city or country; [to] or [tin] are most common:

Check again Unit 14.

I am from…
[íme apó…]
Είμαι από...

...Berlin	...London	..Amsterdam	...Madrid
[to verolíno]	[to londhíno]	[to ámsterdam]	[tin madhríti]
το Βερολίνο	το Λονδίνο	το Άμστερνταμ	την Μαδρίτη
...Germany	...England	...Holland	...Spain
[tin ghermanía]	[tin anglía]	[tin olandhía]	[tin ispanía]
την Γερμανία	την Αγγλία	την Ολλανδία	την Ισπανία

the name of a city…
…the name of a country…

There are many different ways to ask people how they are feeling: How are you? [pos íse / íste]? Πώς είσαι / είστε; How are you doing? [ti kánis / kánete]? Τι κάνεις / κάνετε; How is it going? [pos pái]? Πώς πάει; Here are some phrases people use as a reply.

How are you today?
[pos íste símera]?
Πώς είστε σήμερα;
"Very well" or "pretty good" is [polí kalá] Πολύ καλά in Greek!

Very well	Just fine	So - so	Bad	Terrible
[polí kalá]	[miá hará]	[étsi ki étsi]	[áshima]	[hália]
Πολύ καλά	Μια χαρά	Έτσι κι έτσι	Άσχημα	Χάλια

Post office and bank: Two necessary stops while traveling.

ΤΡΑΠΕΖΑ
*stands for bank
in Greek!*

Greece has replaced its national currency with Euro [evró] Ευρώ in the beginning of 2002. There are eight coins of 1, 2, 5, 10, 50 cents [...] λεπτά and 1 and 2 Euros. There are also seven banknotes of 5, 10, 20, 50, 100, 200 and 500 Euros. All EU member states have introduced Euro so money exchange will be necessary for people coming to Greece from a non-EU country. Some important phrases here:

-What's the exchange rate for...?
[piá íne i timí isotimías ya...]?
Ποια είναι η τιμή ισοτιμίας για...;

- American / Canadian / Australian dollars?
[amerikánika/ kanadhézika / afstralézika dholária]?
αμερικάνικα / καναδέζικα / αυστραλέζικα δολλάρια;

- Where can I cash some traveler's checks?
[pu boró na haláso taxidhiotikés epitaghés]?
Πού μπορώ να χαλάσω ταξιδιωτικές επιταγές;

- Can I charge it on my credit card?
[boro na to hreóso stin pistotikí mu kárta]?
Μπορώ να τα χρεώσω στην πιστωτική μου κάρτα;

- Is there a bank / post office around here?
[ipárhi trápeza / tahidhromío edhó kondá]?
Υπάρχει τράπεζα / ταχυδρομείο εδώ κοντά;

- Can I see your passport please?
[boró na dho to dhiavatírió sas]?
Μπορώ να δω το διαβατήριο σας, παρακαλώ;

*In most banks
you will find
someone who
speaks English!
Money talks...*

The Greek post office ΕΛΤΑ [eltá] is affiliated with Western Union for people who would like to send or receive money in Greece. Opening hours for both banks or post offices differ from city to city and during off-season or high-season. Check to find out the exact times locally.

ΤΑΧΥΔΡΟΜΕΙΟΝ *[tahidhromíon] stands for post office in Greek!*

1. clerk [ipálilos] υπάλληλος
2. mailbox [ghramatokivótio] γραμματοκιβώτιο
3. mailman [tahidhrómos] ταχυδρόμος
4. pen [stiló] στυλό
5. stamp [ghramatósimo] γραμματόσημο
6. display [ékthema] έκθεμα
7. services [ipiresíes] υπηρεσίες
8. address [dhiéfthinsi] διεύθυνση
9. postal code [kodhikós] κωδικός
10. sender [apostoléas] αποστολέας
11. cards [kártes] κάρτες
12. letter [ghráma] γράμμα
13. telegram [tileghráfima] τηλεγράφημα

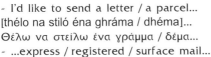

- I'd like to send a letter / a parcel...
[thélo na stiló éna ghráma / dhéma]...
Θέλω να στείλω ένα γράμμα / δέμα...
- ...express / registered / surface mail...
[exprés] [sistiméno] [kanonikó-apló]...
...εξπρές / συστημένο / κανονικό - απλό...
- ...stamps for England / the States...
[...ghramatósima ya tin anglía /ya tin amerikí]...
...γραμματόσημα για την Αγγλία / για την Αμερική...
- One stamp for a postcard inland...
[éna ghramatósimo ya kárta sto esoterikó]...
Ένα γραμματόσημο για κάρτα στο εσωτερικό...

Postcards and stamps can be purchased in several tourist shops or even kiosks [períptera] περίπτερα around Greece!

Minor medical emergencies: Tips for everyday symptoms!

It's always best to have international health insurance coverage while in Greece. We hope that no medical emergency will arise, in which case this book at hand will not be of much value, but small things including sunburns, or asking for an aspirin to take a light headache away can be possible. Remember that almost all hospitals have many doctors who speak English and some of them have even studied in England or the States. In larger cities you'll encounter private and state - run hospitals but in smaller places only public health institutes will be found.

Some symptoms!

1. I've got a cough... [ého víha]... Έχω βήχα...
2. My tummy hurts... [me ponái i kiliá]... Με πονάει η κοιλιά...
3. My eye hurts... [me ponái to máti]... Με πονάει το μάτι...
4. I've got a fever... [ého piretó]... Έχω πυρετό...

My ... hurts!
[me ponái...]
My ... hurt!
[me ponún]

...head	...eyes	...nose	...mouth	...ears
[to kefáli]	[ta mátia]	[i míti]	[to stóma]	[ta aftiá]
το κεφάλι	τα μάτια	η μύτη	το στόμα	τα αυτιά

"Eyes and ears" go with [ponún], the rest with [ponái]!

appendix	[skolikoidhítis]	σκωληκοειδίτης
artery	[artiría]	αρτηρία
bladder	[kísti]	κύστη
blood	[éma]	αίμα
bones	[kókala]	κόκαλα
brain	[mialó]	μυαλό
heart	[kardhiá]	καρδιά
hip	[ghofós]	γοφός
intestine	[éndero]	έντερο
jaws	[saghónia]	σαγόνια
joint	[árthrosi]	άρθρωση
kidneys	[nefrá]	νεφρά
liver	[sikóti]	συκώτι
lung	[pnévmonas]	πνεύμονας
muscle	[mis]	μυς
nerve	[névro]	νεύρο
rib	[plevró]	πλευρό
skin	[dhérma]	δέρμα
tongue	[ghlósa]	γλώσσα
vein	[fléva]	φλέβα

*Some
body parts
and organs.*

*The body
[to sóma]*
Το σώμα

At the pharmacy! [sto farmakío]
Στο Φαρμακείο!

- I'd like some
  eyedrops / eardrops / cough drops.
  [tha íthela staghónes
  ya... ta mátia / ta aftiá / to lemó]
  Θα ήθελα σταγόνες
  για... τα μάτια / τα αυτιά / το λαιμό.
- I need something
  for diarrhea / sun burn!
  [hriazome kati
  ya dhiária / égavma apó ílio]
  Χρειάζομαι κάτι
  για διάρροια / έγκαυμα από ήλιο.
- Do you have bandages
  / pain killers / sleeping pills?
  [éhete epidhézmus
  /pafsípona / ipnotiká hápia]
  Έχετε επιδέσμους
  / παυσίπονα / υπνωτικά χάπια;
- aspirin / medication / prescription
  [aspiríni / fármako / sindaghí]
  ασπιρίνη / φάρμακο / συνταγή

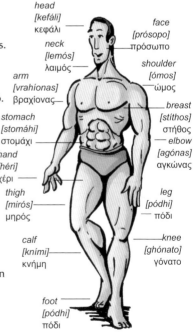

head
[kefáli]
κεφάλι

face
[prósopo]
πρόσωπο

neck
[lemós]
λαιμός

shoulder
[ómos]
ώμος

arm
[vrahíonas]
βραχίονας

breast
[stíthos]
στήθος

stomach
[stomáhi]
στομάχι

elbow
[agónas]
αγκώνας

hand
[héri]
χέρι

thigh
[mirós]
μηρός

leg
[pódhi]
πόδι

knee
[ghónato]
γόνατο

calf
[kními]
κνήμη

foot
[pódhi]
πόδι

Cultural
guide

Cultural guide

This section was written with the intention of making you more aware of the Greek language and culture. It will give you suggestions and ideas for you to explore and try out while in Greece but it won't attempt by any means to limit your imagination, likes, or dislikes. To experience, assimilate, or even accept a new culture and language is not an easy or fast process and it definitely requires an open mind and heart.

Use this cultural guide as a starting point when visiting Greece and we believe that your experiences will be more enriched and rewarding.

Good Luck!

A Where to go!

B What to buy!

C How to understand!

D Who to contact!

E Why bother?

A Where to go!

If you ever ask a Greek where to go or even a foreigner who has visited some places in Greece, the responses will be more diverse than you can imagine! Of course, your personal interests, your local contacts, and your budget will play an important role. Our suggestions and ideas below include archaeological sites, popular tourist destinations, remote, semi - explored places, and national parks.

Cities and towns to visit

Well written city guides are available in English!

Athens [athína] Αθήνα is our first suggestion! Almost half of the Greek population throngs there and the city is well diversified with antiquities next to post - modernistic buildings. Many cultural and research institutes, all ministries and public offices, most major Greek or multinational companies are situated and the majority of state organizations or private corporations have their main offices or headquarters there. Thessalonica [thessaloníki] Θεσσαλονίκη is the second largest city in Greece with almost 1,000,000 people. There you can get a flavor of northern Greece with its cosmopolitan and cultural heritage. Rhodes [ródhos] Ρόδος in the south and Corfu [kérkira] Κέρκυρα in the north-west have been the two most favorite destinations for tourists for the last

forty years! In the nineties many more destinations have enjoyed a considerably larger number of tourists including Chalkidiki [halkidhikí] Χαλκιδική in the north, Sporades islands [sporádhes] Σποράδες in central Greece, the seven-island group [eptánisa] Επτάνησα in western Greece, the Peloponnese [pelopónisos] Πελοπόννησος, the Cycladic islands [kikládhes] Κυκλάδες south of Athens, and Crete [kríti] Κρήτη in the south.
We thought it could have been interesting to create an A-Z guide for you as an extra option to your itenary!

Where to go - What to see

A. ΑΘΗΝΑ - Athens - blend of past and present
B. ΒΕΡΟΙΑ - Veria - Vergina
Γ. ΓΥΘΕΙΟ - The Peloponnese - Sparta, Mystras
Δ. ΔΕΛΦΟΙ - Amfissa - Delphi oracles
E. ΕΡΜΟΥΠΟΛΗ - Syros island - Cycladic art
Z. ΖΑΚΥΝΘΟΣ - Zakynthos island - Solomos anthem
H. ΗΡΑΚΛΕΙΟ - Crete - Knossos
Θ. ΘΕΣΣΑΛΟΝΙΚΗ - Thessalonica - East meets west
I. ΙΩΑΝΝΙΝΑ - Epirus - Dodoni oracles
K. ΚΑΣΤΟΡΙΑ - Kastoria - the fur district
Λ. ΛΑΡΙΣΑ - Larissa - Farsala, Mount Olympus
M. ΜΥΤΙΛΗΝΗ - Lesbos island - petrified forest
N. ΝΑΥΠΛΙΟ - the Peloponnese - Mycenean culture
Ξ. ΞΑΝΘΗ - Xanthi - Orman forest, Avdira
O. ΟΛΥΜΠΙΑ - The Peloponnese - Temple, Praxiteles
Π. ΠΑΤΡΑ - The Peloponnese - 3rd largest city
P. ΡΟΔΟΣ - Rhodes - Lindos, Iallysos, Kamiros
Σ. ΣΑΜΟΣ - Samos island - Pythaghorion
T. ΤΡΙΚΑΛΑ - Trikala - Meteora, Kalambaka
Y. ΥΔΡΑ - Hydra island - Egina, Poros, Spetses
Φ. ΦΙΣΚΑΡΔΟ - Cephalonia island - Assos, Ithaka
X. ΧΑΝΙΑ - Crete - Falasarha, Samaria gorge
Ψ. ΨΑΡΑ - Psara island - Chios, Apollo temple
Ω. ΩΡΑΙΟΚΑΣΤΡΟ - Epirus - Zagoria,...

The A - Z guide of interesting destinations in Greece!

B What to buy!

Best tip!
Ask for
local products
wherever
you go!

"What can I buy in Greece?" is a typical question often asked by many visitors. Again here as in the previous section we cannot prescribe "ideal" buys; what we can suggest though is local artifacts, handicrafts, products well - received, and unique items possibly found in remote villages or downtown Athens! Locals will always tell you proudly of what they produce! Greece is a wine - making country and we believe that many different regions produce high quality table wines, [krasí] κρασί if you have forgotten the word! Hand-made jewelery is also well made; silverware items or even fur pieces if you are not against the idea. You can always be intrigued by an "authentic" item like worry beads [kombolói] κομπολόι! Many tourists enjoy buying a flokati rug [flokáti] φλοκάτη to decorate their walls or floors back home! Simple items will do the job too! A bottle of ouzo [úzo] ούζο, raki [rakí] ρακι, or tsipouro [tsípuro] τσίπουρο can do the trick! Retsina, the resinated wine, found all over Greece or even a bottle of table wine will be sufficient for many who wish to avoid any kind of shopping spree.

Don't pack
anything!
Let them
send it to your
home-address!
Most will
do that!

Anyways, Greece is not for any kind of shopping spree! Right? Below we have again created an *A - Z guide* for people who have shopping in mind! Do not forget we are a consumer's society! Personalize this list and enjoy many possible bargains while in Greece!

What to buy - Where to buy

A - ΑΣΗΜΙΚΑ - Silverware - Epirus n. Greece
B - ΒΙΒΛΙΑ - Books - Athens
Γ - ΓΟΥΝΕΣ - Furs - Kastoria, n. Greece
Δ - ΔΕΡΜΑΤΙΝΑ - Leather ware - n. Greece
E - ΕΙΚΟΝΕΣ - Religious icons - Patmos
Z - ΖΑΧΑΡΩΤΑ - Sweetmeat / candies - Corfu
H - ΗΛΙΟΒΑΣΙΛΕΜΑ - Sunset - Everywhere in Greece
Θ - ΘΑΛΑΣΣΑ - Sea / water - all over Greece
I - ΙΧΘΥΕΣ - Fish - especially on islands
K - ΚΡΑΣΙ - Wine - everywhere
Λ - ΛΑΔΙ - Olive oil - Peloponnese, Crete
M - ΜΑΣΤΙΧΑ - Mastic / Chewing gum - Chios
N - ΝΕΡΟ - Bottled water - everywhere
Ξ - ΞΥΛΟΓΛΥΠΤΑ - Wooden articrafts - Corfu
O - ΟΥΖΟ - Ouzo - Eastern Greece - Mitilini
Π - ΠΗΛΙΝΑ - Clay pottery / ceramics - Rhodes
P - ΡΑΚΙ - Raki - Crete
Σ - ΣΟΥΒΛΑΚΙ - Souvlaki - everywhere
T - ΤΣΙΠΟΥΡΟ - Tsipouro - Western Greece
Y - ΥΑΛΟΓΡΑΦΗΜΑΤΑ - Stained glass - Athens
Φ - ΦΛΟΚΑΤΕΣ - Flokati rugs - Northern Greece
X - ΧΡΥΣΑΦΙΚΑ - Jewelry - Athens, n. Greece
Ψ - ΨΩΜΙ - Bread - Villages all over Greece
Ω - ΩΚΙΜΟΝ / ΜΠΑΧΑΡΙΚΑ - Basil / Herbs - everywhere

Expect to find most items on this list everywhere in Greece. The names of some places indicate that items are produced there locally.

The A - Z guide of interesting shopping ideas.

Sorry! But some things money cannot buy! H + Θ "sunset and sea" are not an exception!

The everyday word for fish is ΨΑΡΙΑ [psária]; for stained glass ΒΙΤΡΩ [vitró],

Who to contact!

Check page 168.

Let your fingers do the walking! Read or skim through some books before and during your visit or stay in Greece. There are several well written books in English about almost all possible subjects including travel books, Greek cooking, architecture, politics, antiquities, museums and many more. Check our pages for some suggestions for further reading.

Check page 166.

There are numerous sites about Greek reality. Our suggestions there can give you some contacts although there are many more and the number increases almost on a weekly basis!

Contact your embassy!

It's always good to have some important addresses and telephone numbers handy while in Greece. We list some English-speaking embassies in Athens below but double check the information when there! People move and telephone numbers change!

United Kingdom - Ploutarhou Str. 1
- 723-6211
United States - Vasilisis Sofias Ave 91
- 721-2951
Australia - Soutsou Str 37
- 644-7303
Republic of Ireland - Vas. Konstantinou 7
- 723-2771

Don't forget to add the area code 210 prefix.

In any emergency, dial 171 for the tourist police; they speak English. In specific emergencies, dial 100 for the Greek police; 104 for a car breakdown; 107 for pharmacies open all night; 150 for the ambulance; 166 for first aid; and 199 for the fire department. Remember that all three-digit numbers do not require any area code. With regard to telephone calls we suggest that you buy a telephone card found in most kiosks and newsstands around Greece when you first arrive. Then you can use it in any public telephone booth which are readily available everywhere. To call home you need to know the country code, city code, and the telephone number. The country code for the UK is 0044; 001 for the United States; 0061 for Australia and 00353 for Ireland.

Before you go to Greece or even while you are there one of your best contacts about travel information around Greece is the Greek National Tourist Organization. GNTO is simply known as EOT [eót] in Greek or Ελληνικός Οργανισμός Τουρισμού. Visit them for brochures and maps in English. Some of their offices are:

Athens - Syntagma Square,
(210) - 323-4130
London - 195 - 197 Regent St.,
(171)-734-5997
New York - 645 Fifth Ave.,
(212)-421-5777
Toronto - 1300 Bay st., (416)-968-2220
Sydney - 51-57 Pitt, St., (2)-241-1663

Highlight these telephone numbers!

I want to call home!

GNTO or simply EOT has offices in many cities in Greece and abroad!

Why bother?

Some good reasons why to bother!

Why do you really have to bother knowing a few things about the Greek language and culture? Perhaps for fun! Perhaps to check out the possibility of embarking on a new language! Perhaps you had a good time on your last visit and you want to be prepared now! "Speechless in Greece" is not fun, is it? We believe so; it's not fun in any place where people cannot speak our language, and we would like to hope that having this book at hand has assisted you in bringing the two languages and cultures closer. After all, many say that Greece is the birthplace of democracy and the cradle of *Western civilization.* It's the place where *drama, comedy, history,* or *philosophy* originated. Greece also invented the Olympic Games which will again take place in Greece in 2004! Ancient Greece created a style of architecture that has been the model for buildings, monuments, and state capitols all over the world. Doctors still take the Hippocratic Oath, named after the father of medicine, Hippocrates. These are just a few reasons why to bother!

Some facts about Greece!

It would have been an oversight not to mention a few things about Greece. Greece occupies about 4% of the EU. The total land area of Greece is about

132,000 km^2 or 52,000 m^2. Three-quarters of this area is the mainland and one quarter is islands. Apart from the north-east where Greece borders with Albania, FYROM, Bulgaria, and Turkey, the rest is about *15,000 km stretch of coast line* including an incredible collection of beaches, bays, coves, harbors, and unexplored or uninhabited seasides. An amazing number of 6,000 different flowers and plants grow in Greece and the sun shines around *3,000 hours yearly!* "Small in size but big In wonders" some people say when talking about this country. And what about *its history?* This is the pride of Greece! Read on!

Timelines	*Events*
3200 - 2200 BC	Bronze Age in Cyclades, Crete
2000 - 1700 BC	First Greek speakers; Golden Age and palaces in Crete
1600 - 1200 BC	Start and end of Mycenaean culture
776 BC	First Olympic Games
500 - 400 BC	Parthenon built; Golden age under Pericles; Drama originates with Aeschylus, Sophocles, Euripides
400 - 300 BC	Plato's Academy founded; Time of Alexander the Great
200 BC - AD 300	The Roman Empire
AD 300 - 1200	Constantinople built; Crusaders
1453 - 1821	Ottoman Empire; Independence
1912 - 1913	Balkan Wars; Territory from Turks
1923 - 1944	World War I and II
1945 - 1949	Civil War; Communists/promonarchy
1967 - 1974	Military junta in power
1974 - present	Democracy returns to Greece.

Check out the most important timelines in Greek history!

Do you know
your ABC's?

Do you know
your ABC's?

The Greek alphabet and some grammar rules: what to bend and what to avoid! This section was written in order to clarify a few things about the Greek alphabet; it will also try to justify and explain the transliteration system used throughout this phrase book; it will finally brief you with "no-frills" and "headache-free" simple explanations regarding some basic grammar rules of the Greek language. Come back to this section often, whenever you want to look up a transliteration or an explanation that makes more sense when applied to the 36 units of this book. Read on and enjoy...

A   The Greek Alphabet

B   Some grammar rules

The Greek alphabet

There are 24 letters in the Greek alphabet: 7 are vowels and 17 consonants.

Finally! The alphabet!

Read also about transliteration on pages 18-21.

Remember that these are approximate sounds!

The sounds of Γ and X might present some difficulties.

GREEK ALPHABET	NAME	TRANSLI-TERATION	PRONUNCIATION
Α α	álfa	[a]	as in raft
Β β	víta	[v]	as in vet
Γ γ (*)	gháma	[gh] or [y]	as in yield or yes
Δ δ	dhélta	[dh]	as in this
Ε ε	épsilon	[e]	as in pet
Ζ z	zíta	[z]	as in zip
Η n	íta	[i]	as in is
Θ ϑ	thíta	[th]	as in thin
Ι ι	yóta	[i]	as in is
Κ κ	káppa	[k]	as in kit
Λ λ	lámdha	[l]	as in let
Μ μ	mi	[m]	as in met
Ν ν	ni	[n]	as in net
Ξ ς	xi	[x]	as in six
Ο ο	ómikron	[o]	as in over
Π π	pi	[p]	as in pet
Ρ ρ	ro	[r]	as in red
Σ σ/ς (*)	síghma	[s] or [z]	as in set or zip
Τ τ	taf	[t]	as in test
Υ υ	ípsilon	[i]	as in is
Φ φ	fi	[f]	as in fit
Χ x (*)	hi	[h] or [ch]	as in hit or as in loch
Ψ ψ	psi	[ps]	as in laps
Ω ω	oméga	[o]	as in over

(*) All three letters marked with an asterisk have two possible pronunciations depending on the letter following.

There are some two-letter combinations which create new sounds.

COMBI-NATIONS	TRANSLI-TERATIONS	PRONUNCIATION
AI αι	[e]	as in pet
EI ει	[i]	as in is
OI οι	[i]	as in is
OY ου	[u]	as in put
AY αυ	[af] or [av]	as in after or as in avenue
EY ευ	[ef] or [ev]	as in left or as in ever
- γγ	[ng]	as in English
- γχ	[nh]	as in inherent
ΓΚ γκ	[g] or [ng]	as in go or as in English
ΜΠ μπ	[b] or [mb]	as in boy or as in timber
NT ντ	[d] or [nd]	as in day or as in end
ΤΣ τσ	[ts]	as in sets
ΤΖ τζ	[dz]	as in adze

Try to see if you can transliterate or write in Greek some words you know!

Be careful of the different sounds of "g" in [g], [gh] and [ng] or of "d" in [d], [dh] and [nd]. The "th" in English is rendered either as [dh] or [th] in Greek

Greek is relatively easy to pronounce because it is, unlike English, a phonetic language. That simply means that you can read or pronounce any word once you know the alphabet, something similar to German, Italian, or Spanish! The accent mark used on Greek words will guide you where to put the stress.

Some grammar rules

This section is too short to make you an expert in a rather complicated system as the Greek grammar! It will attempt though to bring to your attention some rules that make sense to keep in mind when you want to construct some Greek phrases.

Word-order: Is there one?

A Greek sentence can be structured in more than one way, unlike English, placing in first place what speakers want to emphasize. So the English phrase "John loves Mary" can be rendered six different ways in Greek for example! In English, we can change our intonation in order to emphasize, in Greek we can change the word order. Don't worry though, since you can keep the English word order in the phrases you construct.

Articles: Small but important words!

There are three articles in English: the, a, an. Greek, again here, uses many more words to render those three important articles. As a start, this is because the nouns these words define are divided into three genders: masculine, feminine, and neuter. For example the words "the man, the woman, and the child" become [o ándras] ο άντρας, [i ghinéka] η γυναίκα, and [to pedhí] το παιδί! Correspondingly, "a man - a woman - a child" are rendered as "[énas ándras] [mía ghinéka] [éna pedhí].

Greek uses articles with the names of days, months, years, cities, countries or people!

Most languages construct their structure around a verb. In our example "John loves

Mary" the message we receive comes from the word "loves" and we can contrast it to other ideas such as "hits", "pulls", or "kisses". Greek verbs have many more endings compared to English verbs and that allows them often to exclude personal pronouns (Unit 14) altogether. For example, the verb "I have" is rendered in Greek as "[ého] έχω" rather than "[eghóého] εγώ έχω". Similarly, "you have" is "[éhete] έχετε" since it is a different form and there is no any problem of confusion.

Verbs are words that indicate action, being or feeling!

Read Unit 14 again!

Personal pronouns, words like "I, you, he, we, they", are usually omitted with Greek verbs. Possessive pronouns, words like "my, your, his, our" are always necessary and come unlike English after the noun they modify. For example, "my book" is literally "the book my" (!) "[to vivlío mu] το βιβλίο μου in Greek. The article, that is the word "the", is required here! The possessive pronouns are: my [mu] μου, your [su] σου, his [tu] του, her [tis] της, its [tu] του, our [mas] μας, your [sas] σας, and their [tus] τους!

Pronouns: to use or not to use?

Prepositions in English are such words as "in, at, to, with, for", The most common prepositions in Greek are from [apó] από, for [ya] για, with [me] με, without [horís] χωρίς, before [prin] πριν, until [méhri] μέχρι, after [metá] μετά, to [se] σε. Some two-word prepositions: close to [kondá se] κοντά σε, next to [dhípla se] δίπλα σε, far from [makriá apó] μακριά από.

Prepositions: something… easy, at least!

English - Greek
glossary

Greek - English
glossary

120

VI   Glossaries

In this section you will find a list of most everyday words. The two glossaries are limited in size and do not intend to replace a good comprehensive dictionary; they can be handy to consult when you want to look up a word you believe is part of this phrase book. All nouns are marked as (m - f - n) for masculine, feminine, or neuter and correspondingly they go with either [o - i - to] (o, η, το) articles in Greek. All adjectives have also the different endings necessary for masculine - feminine - or neuter.

A   Greek - English glossary

B   English - Greek glossary

A   Greek - English Glossary

Αα	[áa]	(Oh, I get it!)
αγαπάω	[aghapáo]	I love
Αγγλία	[anglía]	England (f)
Αγγλικά	[angliká]	English (language)
αγγουράκι	[anguráki]	small cucumber (n)
αγορά	[agorá]	market (f)
αγροτικός/-ή/-ό	[aghrotikós/-í/-ó]	agricultural
άγχος	[ánhos]	stress (n)
αδιάθετος/-n	[adhiáthetos/-i]	sick (m+f)
αεράκι	[aeráki]	wind (light), breeze (n)
αέρας	[aéras]	wind (m)
αεροδρόμιο	[aerodhrómio]	airport (n)
Αθήνα	[athína]	Athens (f)
Αθηναία	[athinéa]	Athenian (f)
Αθηναίος	[athinéos]	Athenian (m)
αίθουσα	[éthusa]	room, hall (f)
αιτία	[etía]	cause, reason
ακόμα (n)	[akóma]	still, yet
ακούγομαι	[akúghome]	I sound
ακουστικό	[akustikó]	receiver (n)
ακούω	[akúo]	I listen, I hear
ακριβά	[akrivá]	expensively
ακριβός/-ή/-ό	[akrivós/-í/-ó]	expensive
Αλεξάνδρα	[alexándra]	Alexandra (f)
αλήθεια	[alíthia]	truth (f)
αλήθεια!	[alíthia!]	really!, that's true!
αλλά	[alá]	but
αλλεργικός	[alerghikós]	allergic
αλλιώς	[aliós]	otherwise
άλλος/-n/-o	[álos/-i/-o]	other, another
αμέσως	[amésos]	at once
αμμουδιά	[amudhiá]	sand (f)
αν	[án]	if
ανακαινισμένος/-n/-o	[anakenizménos/-i/-o]	renovated
ανανάς	[ananás]	pineapple (m)
αναπαύομαι	[anapávome]	I rest
ανάπαυση	[anápafsi]	rest (f)

Ανάσταση	[anástasi]	Resurrection
ανατολικός/-ή/-ό	[anatolikós/-í-ó]	eastern
άνδρας	[ándras]	man
ανδρικός/-ή/-ό	[andrikós/-í/-ó]	male
ανεβαίνω	[anevéno]	I go up
άνεμος	[ánemos]	wind (m)
ανηφόρα	[anifóra]	uphill (f)
άνηθος	[anithos]	dill (m)
ανοικτός/-ή/-ό	[aniktós/-í/-ó]	light/open
άνοιξη	[ánixi]	spring (f)
αντέχω	[andého]	I stand
αντί	[andí]	instead
αντιβιοτικό	[andiviotikó]	antibiotic (n)
αντισηπτικό	[andisiptikó]	antiseptic (n)
αντίστοιχος/-n/-ο	[andístihos/-i/-o]	corresponding
Αντώνης	[andónis]	Anthony
αξιοθέατο	[axiothéato]	sight (n)
απαισιόδοξος/-n/-ο	[apesiódhoxos/-i/-o]	pessimist
απαίσιος/-α/-ο	[apésios/-a/-o]	awful
απλός/-ή/-ό	[aplós/-í/-ó]	simple
απλά	[aplá]	simply
από	[apó]	from
απορρημένος/-n/-ο	[aporiménos/-i/-o]	confused
αποσκευή	[aposkeví]	luggage, suitcase (f)
αποφασίζω	[apofasízo]	I decide
Απρίλιος /Απρίλης	[aprílios/aprílis]	April (m)
άρα	[ára]	then
αρακάς	[arakás]	pea (m)
αριθμός	[arithmós]	number (m)
αριστερά	[aristerá]	left
αρκετά	[arketá]	enough
αρκετός/-ή/-ό	[arketós/-í/-ó]	several
αρνάκι	[arnáki]	baby lamb (n)
άρρωστος/-n	[árostos/-i]	ill (m+f)
αρχιτέκτονας	[arhitéktonas]	architect (m, f)
ασανσέρ	[asansér]	lift/elevator (n)
ασθενής/-ής/-ές	[asthenís/-ís/-és]	weak
άσθμα	[ásthma]	asthma (n)
άσπρο	[áspro]	white
αστυνομικός	[astinomikós]	policeman (m+f)
άτομο	[átomo]	person (n)

Αύγουστος	[ávghustos]	August (m)
αύξηση	[áfxisi]	increase (f)
αύριο	[ávrio]	tomorrow (n)
αυτοκίνητο	[aftokínito]	car (n)
αυτός/-ή/-ό	[aftós/-í/-ó]	this, he, she, it

B		
βάδην	[vádhin]	walking, jogging (n)
βαθύς/-ιά/-ύ	[vathís]	deep, dark
βαλίτσα	[valítsa]	suitcase (f)
βαριέμαι	[variéme]	I am bored
βάρκα	[várka]	boat (f)
βγάζω	[vgházo]	I take off, pull out
βιβλίο	[vivlío]	book (n)
βιοτικός/-ή/-ό	[viotikós/-i/-ó]	standard (of living)
βλέπω	[vlépo]	I see
βοηθάω	[voitháo]	I help
βόλεϋμπολ	[vóleibol]	volleyball (n)
βορειο-	[vório	
ανατολικός/-ή/-ό	[anatolikós/-í/-ó]	northeastern
βορειοδυτικός/-ή/-ό	[voriodhitikós/-í/-ó]	northwestern
βόρειος/-α/-ο	[vórios /-a/-o]	northern
βοριάς	[voriás]	north winds
βούτυρο	[vútiro]	butter (n)
βρεγμένος/-η/-ο	[vreghménos/-i/-o]	wet
βρίσκω	[vrísko]	I find
βροχή	[vrohí]	rain (f)
βυσσινής/-ιά/-ί	[visinís/-iá/-í]	burgundy
βύσσινο	[vísino]	morel

Γ		
γάλα	[ghála]	milk (n)
γαλάζιο	[ghalázio]	sky blue, indigo
Γαλλία	[ghalía]	France (f)
Γαλλίδα	[ghalída]	French woman (f)
γάμος	[ghámos]	wedding (m)
γάντι	[ghándi]	glove (n)
γεγονός	[gheghonós]	event, fact (n)
γέννηση	[ghénisi]	birth (f)
Γερμανία	[ghermanía]	Germany
Γερμανίδα	[ghermanída]	German woman (f)
γεύμα	[ghévma]	meal (n)
γεύση	[ghéfsi]	taste (f)

γιατί	[yatí]	because /why?
γιατρός	[yatrós]	doctor
γιορτάζω	[yortázo]	I celebrate
γιορτή	[yortí]	holiday (f), celebration
γιωτ	[yot]	yacht (n)
γκαράζ	[garáz]	car park, garage (n)
γκοφρέτα	[gofréta]	waffle (chocolate) (f)
γκρίzος/-α/-ο	[grízos/-a/-o]	grey
γκρινιάζω	[griniázo]	I complain, I moan
γκρουμ	[grum]	porter (m)
γλυκό	[ghlikó]	sweet (n), cake
γλώσσα	[ghlósa]	language (f)
γνωστός/-ή/-ο	[ghnostós/-í/-ó]	acquaintance, known
γραβάτα	[ghraváta]	tie (f)
γραμματόσημο	[ghramatósimo]	stamp (n)
γραμμή	[ghramí]	line (f)
γραφείο	[ghrafío]	office (n)
γράφω	[ghráfo]	I write
γρήγορα	[ghríghora]	fast
γρίπη	[ghrípi]	influenza (f)
γυμναστική	[ghimnastikí]	gymnastics, exercise (f)
γυναίκα	[ghinéka]	woman (f)
γύρος	[ghíros]	gyros (m)
γύρω	[ghíro]	round
γωνία	[ghonía]	corner (f)

δάσκαλος/-α	[dháskalos/-a]	teacher (m/f)
δείχνω	[dhíhno]	I show
Δεκέμβριος	[dhekémvrios]	December (m)
Δεκέμβρης	[dhekémvris]	December (m)
δέντρο	[dhéndro]	tree (n)
δεξιά	[dhexiá]	right
Δευτέρα	[dheftéra]	Monday (f)
δέχομαι	[dhéhome]	I accept
δηλαδή	[dhiladí]	in other words
δηλητηρίαση	[dhilitiríasi]	poisoning (f)
διαβατήριο	[dhiavatírio]	passport (n)
διακοπές	[dhiakopés]	vacation, holidays
διάδρομος	[dhiádhromos]	corridor (m)
διανυκτέρευση	[dhianiktérefsi]	(staying) overnight
διασκεδάζω	[dhiaskedházo]	I entertain (reflexive)

διεύθυνση	[dhiéfthinsi]	address (f)
δίκιο	[dhíkio]	right (n)
δίκλινο	[dhíklino]	double room (n)
δίνω	[dhíno]	I give
διπλός/-ή/-ό	[dhiplós/ -í/-ó]	double
δισκοθήκη	[dhiskothíki]	disco, discotheque
δίσκος	[dhískos]	record (m)
δόση	[dhósi]	installment (f)
δουλειά	[dhuliá]	work, job (f)
δουλεύω	[dhulévo]	I work
δρομολόγιο	[dhromolóyo]	timetable (n)
δρόμος	[dhrómos]	street (m)
δροσερός/-ή/-ό	[dhroserós/-i/-ó]	cool
δυστυχώς	[dhistihós]	unfortunately
δυτικός/-ή/-ό	[dhitikós/-í/-ó]	western
δωμάτιο	[dhomátio]	room (n)
δωρεάν	[dhoreán]	free
δώρο	[dhóro]	present (n)

εγκεφαλικός/-ή/-ό	[egefalikós/-i/-ó]	cerebral
εγώ	[eghó]	I
εδώ	[edhó]	here
εθνικός/-ή/-ό	[ethnikós/-í/-ó]	national
ειδικά	[idhiká]	especially
ειδικός/-ή/-ό	[idhikós/-í/-ó]	specialist, special
εικόνα	[ikóna]	picture (f), icon
είμαι	[íme]	I am
είσοδος	[ísodhos]	entrance (f)
εκεί	[ekí]	there
εκείνος/-η/-ο	[ekínos/-i/-o]	that man/woman/thing
εκπλήσσω	[ekplíso]	I surprise
εκπτωτικός/-ή/-ό	[ekptotikós/-í/-ó]	discount(ed)
Ελλάδα	[eládha]	Greece
Έλληνας	[élinas]	Greek (male)
Ελληνίδα	[elinídha]	Greek (female)
Ελληνικά	[eliniká]	Greek (language)
ελπίζω	[elpízo]	I hope
εμπορικός/-ή/-ό	[emborikós/-í/-ó]	commercial
εντάξει	[endáxi]	all right
ενδιαφέρον	[endhiaféron]	interest (n)
ενοικίαση	[enikíasi]	rent (f)

εντύπωση	[endíposi]	impression (f)
ενυδρείο	[enidhrío]	aquarium (n)
ενώ	[enó]	while, whereas
εξέταση	[exétasi]	examination (f)
έξω	[éxo]	out, outside
εξωτερικό	[exoterikó]	abroad (n)
επάνω	[epáno]	up, above, on
έπειτα	[épita]	afterwards, then
επιθυμώ	[epithimó]	I wish, I desire
επίπεδο	[epípedho]	level (n)
επικίνδυνος/-η/-ο	[epikíndhinos/-i/-o]	dangerous
επίσης	[epísis]	too, also
επιστρέφω	[epistréfo]	I return
επιστροφή	[epistrofí]	return, round trip (f)
επιτέλους!	[epitélus]	at last!
επιτόκιο	[epitókio]	interest (n)
εποχή	[epohí]	season (f)
εργασία	[erghasía]	job, work (f)
εργάτης	[erghátis]	employee, worker (m)
έρχομαι	[érhome]	I come
εσείς	[esís]	you (pl. and fml)
εσένα	[eséna]	you (to /about)
εσύ	[esí]	you (sing. and infml)
εσώρουχο	[esóruho]	underwear
εσωτερικός/-ή/-ό	[esoterikós/-í/-ó]	inner, inside
εταιρία	[etería]	company (f)
ετήσιος/-α/-ο	[etisíos/-a/-o]	annual
έτοιμος/-η/-ο	[étimos/-i/-o]	ready
έτσι	[étsi]	so, like that
ευκαιρία	[efkería]	chance (f)
εύκολα	[éfkola]	easily
εύκολος/-η/-ο	[éfkolos/-i/-o]	easy
Ευρώ	[evró]	Euro (n)
Ευρώπη	[evrópi]	Europe (f)
ευχαριστώ	[efharistó]	(I) thank you
ευχή	[efhí]	wish (f)
εύχομαι	[éfhome]	I wish /I hope
εφημερίδα	[efimerídha]	newspaper (f)
εφιάλτης	[efiáltis]	nightmare (m)
εχθές	[ehthés]	yesterday
έχω	[ého]	I have

7	záλn	[záli]	dizzy (f)
	zaμπóν	[zabón]	ham (n)
	zaχaροπλαστείο	[zaharoplastío]	pastry shop (n)
	zηλεύω	[zilévo]	I become/am jealous
	zωγράφος	[zoghráfos]	painter (m, f)
	zωή	[zoí]	life (f)

H	ή	[i]	or
	η	[i]	the (female article)
	ήδη	[ídhi]	already
	ήλιος	[ílios]	sun (m)
	ημικρανία	[imikranía]	migraine (f)
	ήρεμος/-η/-ο	[íremos/-i /-o]	tranquil
	ήσυχος/-η/-ο	[ísihos/-i/-o]	quiet

Θ	θαλαμηγός	[thalamighós]	yacht (f)
	θάλασσα	[thálasa]	sea (f)
	θαλασσής/-ιά/-ί	[thalasís/-iá /-í]	sea blue
	θάνατος	[thánatos]	death (m)
	θαυμάσιος/-ια/ -ιο	[thavmásios/-ia/-io]	marvelous
	θεά	[theá]	goddess (f)
	θέα	[théa]	view (f)
	θέλω	[thélo]	I want /like
	Θεός	[theós]	God (m)
	θεραπεία	[therapía]	treatment (f)
	θέρετρο	[théretro]	resort (n)
	θερμοκρασία	[thermokrasía]	temperature (f)
	θερμότερος/-η/-ο	[thermóteros/-i/-o]	warmer
	Θεσσαλονίκη	[thesaloníki]	Thessaloniki /Salonica
	θέση	[thési]	class, seat (f)
	θύελλα	[thíela]	storm, hurricane (f)
	θυμάμαι	[thimáme]	I remember

I	ιδιωτικός/-ή/-ό	[idhiotikós/-i/-ó]	private
	Ιανουάριος/Γενάρης	[ianuários/ghenáris]	January (m)
	ίδιος/-α/-ο	[ídhios/-ia /-io]	similar
	ιδίως	[idhíos]	especially
	Ιονικός/-ή/-ό	[ionikós/-i/-ó]	Ionian
	Ιούλιος/Ιούλης	[iúlios / iúlis]	July (m)
	ιππασία	[ipasía]	horseback riding (f)
	ισόγειο	[isóyo]	ground floor (n)

ιστιοπλοΐα	[istioploía]	sailing (f)
ιστιοφόρο	[istiofóro]	sailing boat (n)
ιστορία	[istoría]	story, history (f)
ισχυρός/-ή/-ό	[ishirós/-í/-ó]	strong
ίσως	[ísos]	maybe, perhaps
Ιταλία	[italía]	Italy
Ιταλικά	[italiká]	Italian (language)
Ιταλός	[italós]	Italian (m)
Ιταλίδα	[italídha]	Italian (f)
ιώδες	[iódhes]	violet (n)

κτίριο	[ktírio]	building (n)
καθηγητής	[kathighitís]	teacher, tutor (m)
καθόλου	[kathólu]	not at all
κάθομαι	[káthome]	I sit /stay
και	[ke]	and
και τα δυο	[ke ta dhío]	both
καινούργιος/-ια/-ιο	[kenúrios/-ia/-io]	new
καιρός	[kerós]	time /weather
καλά	[kalá]	well, fine, good, O.K.
καλαμπόκι	[kalambóki]	corn (n)
καλλυντικά	[kalindiká]	cosmetics (pl.)
κάλτσα	[káltsa]	sock (f)
καλύτερος/-η/-ο	[kalíteros/-i/-o]	better
καλώς ορίσατε!	[kalós orísate!]	welcome!
καμαριέρα	[kamariéra]	maid (f)
καναπές	[kanapés]	sofa
κανέλα	[kanéla]	cinnamon (f)
κανελής/-ιά/-ί	[kanelís/-iá/-í]	cinnamon red
κανένας/καμία	[kanénas/kamía	nobody (m, f,)
κανένα	/kanéna]	nothing (n)
κανό	[kanó]	canoe (n)
κάνω	[káno]	I do /I make
καλοκαίρι	[kalokéri]	summer (n)
καπετάνιος	[kapetánios]	captain (m)
καράβι	[karávi]	ship (n)
καραβοκύρης	[karavokíris]	skipper (m)
καραμέλα	[karaméla]	candy (f)
καραφάκι	[karafáki]	small carafe
καρδιακός/-ή/-ό	[kardhiakós/-í/-ó]	cardiac
καρέκλα	[karékla]	chair (f)

καρκίνος	[karkínos]	cancer (m)
καρό	[karó]	checkered
καρότο	[karóto]	carrot (n)
κάρτα	[kárta]	card (f)
καρύδα	[karídha]	coconut (f)
κάστρο	[kástro]	castle (n)
καταιγίδα	[kateghída]	(thunder) storm (f)
καταλαβαίνω	[katalavéno]	I understand
κατάλογος	[katáloghos]	catalogue, list, menu
κάτοικος	[kátikos]	inhabitant, resident
κατσικάκι	[katsikáki]	kid - baby goat (n)
κάτω	[káto]	down, under
καφέ	[kafé]	brown
καφενείο	[kafenío]	coffee place (n)
καφές	[kafés]	coffee (m)
καφετής/-ιά/-ί	[kafetís/-iá/-í]	coffee brown
κεραμιδής/-ιά/-ί	[keramidhís/-iá/-í]	brick red
κεραμίδι	[keramídhi]	tile (n)
κεράσι	[kerási]	cherry (n)
κέρινος/-η/-ο	[kérinos/-i/-o]	wax
κεφάλι	[kefáli]	head (n)
κιλό	[kiló]	kilo (n)
κίνηση	[kínisi]	traffic (f), movement
κιόλας	[kiólas]	already
κίτρινο	[kítrino]	yellow (n)
κλασικός/-ή/-ό	[klasikós/-í/-ó]	classic
κλειδί	[klidhí]	key (n)
κλειστοφοβία	[klistofovía]	claustrophobia (f)
κλιματιζόμενος/-η/-ο	[klimatizomenos]	air - conditioned
κόβω	[kóvo]	I cut
κοιλιά	[kiliá]	belly (f)
κοιλόπονος	[kilóponos]	stomach ache (m)
κόκκινο	[kókino]	red
κολοκύθι	[kolokíthi]	squash (n)
κολόνια	[kolónia]	perfume (f)
κολυμπώ	[kolimbó]	I swim
κολύμπι	[kolímbi]	swimming (n)
κοντά	[kondá]	near/close to
κοντινένταλ	[kondinéndal]	continental
κόπωση	[kóposi]	exhaustion (f)
κορτιζόνη	[kortizóni]	cortisone (f)

κόσμος	[kózmos]	people, crowd (m)
κοσμοσυρροή	[kozmosiroí]	crowd, throng (f)
κότ(τ)ερο	[kótero]	cutter(n)/ speed boat
κουνουπίδι	[kunupídhi]	cauliflower (n)
κουρασμένος/-η/-ο	[kurazménos/-i/-o]	tired
κουρτίνα	[kurtína]	curtain (f)
κουστούμι	[kustúmi]	suit (n)
κρατάω(ώ)	[kratáo(ó)]	I keep
κράτηση	[krátisi]	reservation (f)
κρατικός/-ή/-ό	[kratikós/-í/-ó]	state
κρέας	[kréas]	meat (n)
κρέμα	[kréma]	cream (f)
κρεμμύδι	[kremídhi]	onion (n)
κρουαζιερόπλοιο	[kruazieróplio]	cruise ship (n)
κρύο	[krío]	cold (n)
κρύωμα	[kríoma]	cold (n)
κτηνίατρος	[ktiníatros]	vet (m, f)
κτίριο	[ktírio]	building (n)
κτίστης	[ktístis]	builder (m)
κτυπώ	[ktipó]	I hit
κυλιόμενος/-η/-ο	[kiliómenos/-i/-o]	rolling, on rollers
κυπαρισσής/-ιά/-ί	[kiparisís/-iá/-í]	cypress green
κυπαρίσσι	[kiparísi]	cypress (n)
κυρ'	[kir]	Mr. (informal)
Κυριακή	[kiriakí]	Sunday (f)
κύριος	[kírios]	Mr., gentleman
κυρίως	[kiríos]	mainly
κωπηλασία	[kopilasía]	rowing (f)

λέω	[léo]	I say
λάθος	[láthos]	mistake (n), false
λαϊκός/-ή/-ό	[laikós/-í/-ó]	popular
λαιμός	[lemós]	throat (n)
λάμπα	[lámba]	lamp (f)
λαχανής/-ιά/-ί	[lahanís/-iá/-í]	cabbage green
λαχανικό	[lahanikó]	vegetable (n)
λάχανο	[láhano]	cabbage (n)
λέγομαι	[léghome]	my name is
λεμονάδα	[lemonádha]	lemonade (f)
λεμόνι	[lemóni]	lemon (n)
λεπτό	[leptó]	minute (n)

λέσχη	[léshi]	club (f)
λεφτά	[leftá]	money (pl.)
λιακάδα	[liakádha]	sunshine (f)
λίγος/-η/-ο	[líghos/-i/-o]	some, little
λιμένας	[liménas]	port (m)
λογιστής	[loghistís]	book keeper (m)
λοιπόν	[lipón]	then, well
λόμπυ	[lóbi]	lobby (n)
Λονδίνο	[londhíno]	London (n)
λουλουδάτο	[luludháto]	flowery, floral

M

μάγειρας	[mághiras]	cook (m)
μαζί	[mazí]	together, with
μαθαίνω	[mathéno]	I learn
μαθητής, μαθήτρια	[mathitís, mathítria]	student (m, f)
μαϊντανός	[maindanós]	parsley (m)
Μάιος/Μάης	[máios / máis]	May (m)
μακάρι	[makári]	I wish, if only
μακριά	[makriá]	far
μάλλον	[málon]	rather, probably
μάνατζερ	[mánatzer]	manager (m, f)
μαρμελάδα	[marmeládha]	marmalade (f)
μαρούλι	[marúli]	lettuce (n)
Μάρτιος/Μάρτης	[mártios/mártis]	March (m)
μας	[mas]	our
ματώνω	[matóno]	I bleed
μαύρο	[mávro]	black
μαχαιρώνω	[maheróno]	I knife, stab
με	[me]	with
μεγάλος/-η/-ο	[meghálos/-i/-o]	large
μεγαλύτερος/-η/-ο	[meghalíteros/-i/-o]	larger
Μέγαρο Μουσικής	[mégharo musikís]	Music Hall (m)
μέγεθος	[méghethos]	size (n)
μεζεδοπωλείο	[mezedhopolío]	tavern with a selection of appetizers (n)
μεζές	[mezés]	snacks, starters (m)
μεθαύριο	[methávrio]	the day after tomorrow
μειώνω	[mióno]	I reduce
μελιτζάνα	[melitzána]	aubergine, eggplant
μελιτζανοσαλάτα	[melidzanosaláta]	eggplant dip (f)

μένω	[méno]	I live, I stay
μερικός/-ή/-ό	[merikós/-í/-ó]	some
μέρος	[méros]	place (n)
μέσα	[mésa]	in, inside
μεσαίος/-α/-ο	[meséos/-a/-o]	medium
μετά	[metá]	after, afterwards
μετάβαση	[metávasi]	transport (f)
μετακίνηση	[metakínisi]	transport (f)
μεταξύ	[metaxí]	between
μέτρο	[métro]	meter (n)
μέχρι	[méhri]	until
μήλο	[mílo]	apple (n)
μηχανή	[mihaní]	machine (f)
μία /μια	[mía / miá]	one, a, an
μικρός/-ή/-ό	[mikrós/-í/-ó]	small
μιλάω(ώ)	[miláo] [miló]	I speak
μίνι - μπαρ	[míni -bar]	mini - bar (n)
μ.μ.	[metá mesimvría]	p.m.
μόλις	[mólis]	just
μολύβι	[molívi]	pencil (n)
μόνο	[móno]	only
μονόκλινο	[monóklino]	one bed room (n)
μονόχρωμος/-η/-ο	[monóhromos/-i/-o]	single colour
μου	[mu]	my /me
μουσακάς	[musakás]	moussaka (m)
μουστάρδα	[mustárdha]	mustard (f)
μουσταρδής/ιά/-ί	[mustardhís/-iá/-í]	mustard yellow
μπα!	[ba!]	wow! oh!
μπαλκόνι	[balkóni]	balcony (n)
μπανάνα	[banána]	banana (f)
μπανιέρα	[baniéra]	bathtub (f)
μπάνιο	[bánio]	swimming (n) /bath
μπαρ	[bar]	bar, pub (n)
μπάρμπεκιου	[bárbekiu]	barbeque (n)
μπάσκετμπολ	[básketbol]	basketball (n)
μπερδεύω	[berdhévo]	I mix up
μπλε	[ble]	blue
μπορώ	[boró]	I can
μπουάτ	[buát]	night club (f)
μπουκάλι	[bukáli]	bottle (n)
μπουφές	[bufés]	buffet (m)

μπροστά	[brostá]	in front
μπύρα	[bíra]	beer (f)
μπυραρία	[biraría]	ale-house, pub (f)
μυστικό	[mistikó]	secret (n)
μωβ	[mov]	violet
μώλος	[molós]	pier (m)

N

νοικοκυρά	[nikokirá]	housewife
να!	[na!]	there!
ναι!	[ne!]	yes, hello (on the phone)
νάιτ κλαμπ	[náit klab]	night club (n)
νάτο! να το!	[náto!]	here it is!
ναύτης	[náftis]	sailor (m)
ναυτία	[naftía]	sea sickness, nausea
νερό	[neró]	water (n)
νεφελώδης/-ης/-ες	[nefelódhis/-is/-es]	cloudy, overcast
νέφος	[néfos]	cloud, smog (n)
νησί	[nisí]	island (n)
Νοέμβριος	[noémvrios]	November
Νοέμβρης	[noémvris]	November
νομίζω	[nomízo]	I think
νορμάλ	[normál]	normally
νοσοκομείο	[nosokomío]	hospital (n)
νοσοκόμος/-α	[nosokómos/-a]	nurse (m, f)
νόστιμος/-η/-ο	[nóstimos/-i/-o]	tasty
νοστιμότατος/-η/-ο	[nostimótatos/-i/-o]	most delicious
νούμερο	[número]	number, size (n)
ντολμαδάκια	[dolmadhákia]	dolmadakia
ντομάτα	[domáta]	tomato (f)
ντόπιος/-ια/-ιο	[dópios/ia/-io]	local
ντους	[duz]	shower (n)

Ξ

ξανά	[xaná]	again
ξαναβλέπω	[xanavlépo]	I see again
ξεκινώ	[xekinó]	I start
ξενοδοχείο	[xenodhohío]	hotel (n)
ξένος/-η/-ο	[xénos/-i/-o]	foreign(er)
ξέρω	[xéro]	I know
ξεχνώ	[xehnó]	I forget
ξηρά	[xirá]	ashore (f)

ξιφασκία	[xifaskía]	fencing (f)
ξυράφι	[xiráfi]	razor (n)

οδηγός	[odhighós]	driver (m, f)
οδοντογιατρός	[odhondoyatrós]	dentist (m, f)
οικισμός	[ikizmós]	settlement (m)
Οκτώβριος	[októvrios]	October (m)
Οκτώβρης	[októvris]	October (m)
όλοι	[óli]	everyone
όλος/-η/-ο	[ólos /-i /-o]	everything
ομελέτα	[omeléta]	omelet (f)
ομοιότητα	[omiótita]	resemblance (f)
ομοίωμα	[omíoma]	model (n), image,
όμορφος/-η/-ο	[ómorfos/-i/-o]	beautiful
ομπρέλα	[ombréla]	umbrella (f)
όμως	[ómos]	but, though
ονομάζομαι	[onomázome]	my name is
όπως	[ópos]	as, like
οπωσδήποτε	[oposdhípote]	definitely
οργανισμός	[orghanizmós]	organization
Ορίστε!	[oríste]	Here you go!
όροφος	[órofos]	floor (m)
Ο.Σ.Ε.	[osé]	Greek Interail
όσο	[óso]	as much as
ό,τι	[óti]	whatever
ουζερί	[uzerí]	ouzeri (n)
ούζο	[úzo]	ouzo (n)
ουίσκι	[uíski]	whisky
ουρανής/-ιά/-ί	[uranís/-iá/-í]	sky blue
ουρανός	[uranós]	sky (m)
ούτε	[úte]	not even
ούτε ...ούτε	[úte ...úte]	neither ...nor
ουφ!	[uf!]	Phew!
οφείλω	[ofílo]	I owe
όχι	[óhi]	no

παγάκι	[pagháki]	ice cube (n)
πάγκος	[pángos]	counter (m)
πάγος	[pághos]	ice (m)
παγωνιά	[paghoniá]	frost (f)
παγωτό	[paghotó]	ice cream (n)

παθαίνω	[pathéno]	I suffer
παιδί	[pedhí]	child (n)
παίρνω	[pérno]	I take
πάλι	[páli]	again
παλιόκαιρος	[paliókeros]	awful weather (m)
παλτό	[paltó]	coat (n)
πανηγύρι	[panighíri]	(religious) fair (n)
πάντα	[pánda]	always
παντού	[pandú]	everywhere
πάνω	[páno]	on the top /on /over
παραδοσιακός/-ή/-ό	[paradhosiakós/-i/-o]	traditional
παρακαλώ	[parakaló]	please [read p. 69]
παραλία	[paralía]	beach (f)
παραμονή	[paramoní]	stay (f) /eve (f)
παραπάνω	[parapáno]	more than
Παρασκευή	[paraskeví]	Friday (f)
παράσταση	[parástasi]	performance (f)
παραχρόνου	[parahrónu]	the year after next
παρέα	[paréa]	company (f)
Παρίσι	[parísi]	Paris (n)
πάρκο	[párko]	park (n)
παρόμοιος/-α/-ο	[parómios/-a/-o]	similar
πατάτα	[patáta]	potato (f)
πατινάζ	[patináz]	ice-skating (n)
πάω	[páo]	I go
Πέμπτη	[pémpti]	Thursday (f)
πενήντα	[peninda]	fifty (50)
πενικιλίνη	[penikilíni]	penicillin (f)
πέντε	[pénde]	five
πεπόνι	[pepóni]	melon (n)
περαστικός	[perastikós]	passer-by (m)
περιοδικά	[periodhiká]	periodically
περιοδικό	[periodhikó]	magazine (n)
περίπου	[perípu]	about, roughly
περίπτερο	[períptero]	kiosk, news stand
περνάω (ώ)	[pernáo (ó)]	I pass
περπατάω	[perpatáo]	I walk
πέρσι	[pérsi]	last year
πετάω(ώ)	[petáo (ó)]	I fly, I throw
πέφτω	[péfto]	I fall
πηγαίνω	[pighéno]	I go

πια	[piá]	already/anymore
πιανίστας	[pianístas]	pianist (m)
πιάνω	[piáno]	I catch, I hold
πίκλα	[píkla]	pickle (f)
πιλότος	[pilótos]	pilot (m, f)
πίνακας	[pínakas]	statistical table (m)
πιο	[pió]	more
πιστεύω	[pistévo]	I believe
πίστη	[písti]	credit (f)/faith (f)
πιστωτικός/-ή/-ό	[pistotikós /-i/-ó]	credit
πίσω	[píso]	behind, back
πίτα / πίττα	[píta]	pitta bread
πλατεία	[platía]	square (f)
πληθυντικός	[plithindikós]	plural (m)
πλήρης/-ης/-ες	[plíris/-is/-es]	complete
πληροφορία	[pliroforia]	information (f)
πλοίο	[plío]	ship (n)
π.μ.	[pro mesimvrías]	a.m.
πνευμονία	[pnevmonía]	pneumonia (f)
ποδηλασία	[podhilasía]	cycling (f)
ποδόσφαιρο	[podhósfero]	soccer (n)
ποικιλία	[pikilía]	selection (f)
ποιος/-α/-ο	[piós/-á/-ó]	who, which
ποιότητα	[piótita]	quality (f)
πόλη	[póli]	town (f)
πολύ	[polí]	much, very
πολυκατάστημα	[polikatástima]	department store (n)
πονάω	[ponáo]	I hurt
πονοκέφαλος	[ponokéfalos]	headache (m)
πονόκοιλος	[ponókilos]	tummy ache (m)
πονόλαιμος	[ponólemos]	sore throat (m)
πόνος	[pónos]	pain (m)
πορτοκαλής/-ιά/-ί	[portokalís/-iá/-í]	orange
πορτοκάλι	[portokálí]	orange (n)
πόσο;	[póso?]	how much?
ποτέ	[poté]	never
πότε;	[póte?]	when?
που	[pu]	that/who/which
πού;	[pu?]	where?
πουά	[puá]	spotted, dotted
πουθενά	[puthená]	nowhere, anywhere

πουκάμισο	[pukámiso]	shirt (n)
πουλόβερ	[pulóver]	sweater (n)
πράγματι	[prághmati]	indeed
πράσινο	[prásino]	green
πριν	[prin]	before
πρόγραμμα	[próghrama]	schedule (n)
πρόπερσι	[própersi]	the year before last
προς	[pros]	to, towards
προσπαθώ	[prospathó]	I try
προσφέρω	[prosféro]	I offer
προσφορά	[prosforá]	offer (f)
πρόσωπο	[prósopo]	face (n)
πρωινό	[proinó]	breakfast (n)
πρώτος/-η/-ο	[prótos/-i/-o]	first
πτήση	[ptísi]	flight (f)
πτώση	[ptósi]	decrease, fall (f)
πω! πω!	[po! po!]	wow!
πως!	[pos!]	of course!
πως;	[pos?]	how? what?

P

ράδιο	[rádhio]	radio (n)
ραντεβού	[randevú]	appointment (n)
ρεσεψιόν	[resepsión]	reception desk (f)
ρεσεψιονίστας	[resepsionístas]	receptionist (m)
ρετσίνα	[retsína]	resinated wine (f)
ριγέ	[righé]	striped
ροδάκινο	[rodhákino]	peach (n)
ρολόι	[rolói]	watch, clock
ρωτάω (ώ)	[rotáo/rotó]	I ask

Σ

στην	[stin]	into, to the
Σάββατο	[sávato]	Saturday (n)
Σαββατοκύριακο	[savatokíriako]	weekend (n)
σαν	[san]	as, like
σάντουϊτς	[sánduits]	sandwich (n)
σας	[sas]	your/you
σεισμός	[sizmós]	earthquake (m)
σέλινο	[sélino]	celery (n)
σεμινάριο	[seminário]	seminar (n)
Σεπτέμβριος	[septémvrios]	September (m)
Σεπτέμβρης	[septémvris]	September (m)

σερβιτόρα	[servitóra]	waitress (f)
σερβιτόρος	[servitóros]	waiter (m)
σέρβις	[sérvis]	room service (n)
σήμερα	[símera]	today
σιγά	[sighá]	slowly
σίγουρος/-η/-ο	[síghuros/-i/-o]	sure
σιέλ	[siél]	sky blue
σινεμά	[sinemá]	cinema (n)
σκάλα	[skála]	staircase (f)
σκαλοπάτι	[skalopáti]	step (n)
σκάφος	[skáfos]	motor boat (n)
σκέπτομαι	[sképtome]	I think
σκέτο	[skéto]	straight
σκι	[ski]	skiing (n)
σκοντάφτω	[skondáfto]	I trip over
σκούρος/-α/-ο	[skúros /-a/-o]	dark
σοβαρός/-ή/-ό	[sovarós/-í/-ó]	serious
σοκολάτα	[sokoláta]	chocolate (f)
σοκολατής/-ιά/-ί	[sokolatís/-iá/-í]	chocolate brown
σου	[su]	to you / you (sing.)
σου	[su]	your
σουβλάκι	[suvláki]	souvlaki (n)
σουίτα	[suíta]	suite (f)
σουτζουκάκια	[sutzukákia]	spicy meat balls
σπάνια	[spánia]	rarely, seldom
σπάω	[spáo]	I break
σπίτι	[spíti]	house (n)
στατιστικός/-ή/-ό	[statistikós/-í/-ó]	statistical
σταφύλι	[stafíli]	grape (n)
στάχτη	[stáhti]	ash (f)
σταχτής/-ιά/ -ί	[stahtís/-iá/-í]	ash grey
στεγνώνω	[steghnóno]	I dry up
στεναχωριέμαι	[stenahoriéme]	I worry
στεναχωρημένος	[stenahoriménos]	worried, troubled
στης	[stis]	at (the) / on-in-to
στο	[sto]	at (the) / on-in-to
στοιχεία	[stihía]	data
στυλό	[stiló]	pen (n)
συγγνώμη	[sighnómi]	excuse me
συμβουλή	[simvulí]	advice (f)
συμπληρώνω	[simbliróno]	I fill out

συνάδελφος	[sinádhelfos]	colleague (m, f)
συνάλλαγμα	[sinalághma]	exchange (n)
συναρπαστικός	[sinarpastikós]	unique, exciting
συνέδριο	[sinédhrio]	conference (n)
συνεργασία	[sinerghasía]	cooperation (f)
συνέχεια	[sinéhia]	continually
συνηθίzω	[sinithízo]	I get used to
συνήθως	[siníthos]	usually
σύννεφο	[sínefo]	cloud (n)
συνταγή	[sindaghí]	prescription (f)
συνταξιούχος	[sindaxiúhos]	retiree (m, f)
σύντομα	[síndoma]	shortly, soon
σύστημα	[sístima]	system (n)
συχνά	[sihná]	often, frequently
σφαιροβολία	[sferovolía]	shot-put (f)
σχεδιάzω	[shedhiázo]	I plan / I design
σχεδόν	[shedhón]	almost
σχεδόν ποτέ	[shedhón poté]	hardly ever

Τ		
ταβέρνα	[tavérna]	tavern (f)
ταραγμένος/-η/-ο	[taraghménos/-i/-o]	rough / upset
ταραμοσαλάτα	[taramosálata]	egg - fish salad (f)
τελειώνω	[telióno]	I complete, I end
τελικά	[teliká]	at the end, finally
τέλος	[télos]	end (n)
τέσσερις	[téseris]	four
Τετάρτη	[tetárti]	Wednesday (f)
τέτοιος/-α/-ο	[tétios/-a/-o]	such (a)
τετράκλινο	[tetráklino]	four beds (n)
τζατζίκι	[dzadzíki]	tzatziki (n)
τηλέφωνο	[tiléfono]	telephone (n)
την	[tin]	her
της	[tis]	her
τι	[ti]	what, how
τιμή	[timí]	price (f)
τίποτα	[típota]	nothing / not at all!
τμήμα	[tmíma]	section (n)
το	[to]	the (n)
τοπικός/-ή/-ό	[topikós/-í/-ó]	local
τόσος/-η/-ο	[tósos/-i/-o]	so, so much, so big
τότε	[tóte]	then

του	[tu]	his (m), its (n) / him
τουαλέτα	[tualéta]	toilet (f)
τουλάχιστο(ν)	[tuláhiston]	at least
τουρτουρίζω	[turturízo]	I am shaking
τους	[tus]	their
τράπεζα	[trápeza]	bank (f)
τραπεζικός/-ή/-ό	[trapezikós/-í/-ó]	banking
τρέμω	[trémo]	I shiver
τρέχω	[trého]	I run
τρανταφυλλής/-ιά/-ί	[triandafilís /-iá/-í]	pink
τριαντάφυλλο	[triandáfilo]	rose (n)
τριήμερο	[triímero]	long weekend
τρίκλινο	[tríklino]	three beds (n)
τρικυμία	[trikimía]	storm, tempest (f)
Τρίτη	[tríti]	Tuesday (f)
τρομερό!	[tromeró]	awesome! / awful!
τρομερός/-ή/-ό	[tromerós/-í/-ó]	awful, terrible
τροφή	[trofí]	food (f)
τροχάδην	[trohádhin]	running (n)
τροχός	[trohós]	wheel (m)
τρώω	[tróo]	I eat
τσάι	[tsái]	tea (n)
τσάντα	[tsánda]	bag (f)
τσίκλα	[tsíkla]	chewing gum (f)
τυρί	[tirí]	cheese (n)
τώρα	[tóra]	now

υπάλληλος	[ipálilos]	officer, clerk (m, f)
υπάρχει / υπάρχουν	[ipárhi/ipárhun]	there is / there are
υγεία	[ighía]	health (f)
υγρασία	[ighrasía]	humidity (f)
υπεραστικός/-ή/-ό	[iperastikós/-í/-ó]	long distance
υπερκόπωση	[iperkóposi]	overexhaustion
υπέροχος/-η/-ο	[ipérohos/-i/-o]	excellent
υπόγειο	[ipóghio]	cellar (n) / basement
υπόλοιπος/-η/-ο	[ipólipos/-i/-o]	rest, remaining
ύστερα	[ístera]	later on, afterwards
υψηλός/-ή/-ό	[ipsilós/-í/-o]	high

φαίνομαι	[fénome]	I look
φάκελος	[fákelos]	envelope (m)

φανάρι	[fanári]	traffic light (n)
φανταστικό!	[fandastikó]	fantastic!
φαρδύς/-ιά/-ύ	[fardhís/-iá/-í]	wide
φαρμακείο	[farmakío]	pharmacy / chemist's
φάρμακο	[fármako]	medicine (n)
φαρμακοποιός	[farmakopiós]	chemist / pharmacist
Φεβρουάριος	[fevruários]	February (m)
Φλεβάρης	[fleváris]	February (m)
φεύγω	[févgho]	I leave
φημισμένος/-η/-ο	[fimizménos/-i/-o]	famous
φθινόπωρο	[fthinóporo]	fall, autumn (n)
φιλικότερος/-η/-ο	[filikóteros/-i/-o]	friendlier
φίλος/φίλη	[fílos] [fíli]	friend (m, f)
φοράω (ώ)	[foráo/foró]	I wear
φόρεμα	[fórema]	dress (n)
φουαγιέ	[fuayé]	foyer (n)
φούστα	[fústa]	skirt (f)
Φ.Π.Α	[fi-pi-a]	V.A.T.
φράουλα	[fráula]	strawberry (f)
φρούτο	[frúto]	fruit (n)
φρυγανιά	[frighaniá]	rusk (f)
φτηνός/-ή/-ό	[ftinós/-í/-ó]	cheap
φυλασσόμενος/-η/-ο	[filasómenos /-i/-o]	guarded
φυσικά	[fisiká]	of course, certainly
φωνάζω	[fonázo]	I call
φωτογραφία	[fotoghrafía]	photo (f)

X		
χαίρετε	[hérete]	hello (formal)
χαιρετίσματα	[heretízmata]	greetings, regards
χαίρομαι	[hérome]	I am glad
χαλάζι	[halázi]	hail (n)
χαρτοφύλακας	[hartofílakas]	briefcase (m)
χαλασμένος/-η/-ο	[halazménos/-i/-o]	out of order
χάμπουργκερ	[hámburger]	hamburger (n)
χάντμπολ	[hándbol]	handball (n)
χάνω	[háno]	I miss
χάπι	[hápi]	pill (n)
χάρτης	[hártis]	map (m)
χαρτί	[hartí]	paper (n)
χειμώνας	[himónas]	winter (m)
χθες	[hthes]	yesterday

χιόνι	[hióni]	snow (n)
χλωμός/-ή/-ό	[hlomós/-í/-ó]	pale
χμ!	[hm!]	hm!
χορεύω	[horévo]	I dance
χόρτα	[hórta]	greens
χουρμάς	[hurmás]	date (m) (fruit)
χρειάζομαι	[hriázome]	I need
χρυσαφικά	[hrisafiká]	jewellery
χρησιμοποιώ	[hrisimopió]	I use
χρόνος	[hrónos]	year (m)/time
χρώμα	[hróma]	colour (n)
χτες	[htes]	yesterday
χυμός	[himós]	juice (m)
χώρα	[hóra]	country (f)
χώρος	[hóros]	site, space, area (m)

Ψ

ψαράς	[psarás]	fisherman (m)
ψάρι	[psári]	fish (n)
ψαρόβαρκα	[psaróvarka]	fishing boat (f)
ψαροταβέρνα	[psarotavérna]	fish tavern (f)
ψάχνω	[psáhno]	I look for
ψιχάλα	[psihála]	drizzle (f)
ψυγείο	[psighío]	refrigerator (n)
ψωμί	[psomí]	bread (n)
ψώνια	[psónia]	shopping (pl.)

Ω

ωραία	[oréa]	nice, wonderful
ωραίος/-α /-ο	[oréos/-a/-o]	beautiful

B English - Greek Glossary

A		
a.m.	[pro mesimvrías]	π.μ.
a-an / one	[énas], [mía], [éna]	ένας, μία, ένα
about	[perípu]	περίπου
across	[apénandi]	απέναντι
adventure (f)	[peripétia]	περιπέτεια
Aegina (f)	[éghina]	Αίγινα
afterwards	[metá]	μετά
again	[páli]	πάλι
agree	[simfonó]	συμφωνώ
airplane (n)	[aeropláno]	αεροπλάνο
airport (n)	[aerodhrómio]	αεροδρόμιο
almost	[shedhón]	σχεδόν
along	[mazí]	μαζί
always	[pánda]	πάντα
America (f)	[amerikí]	Αμερική
and	[ke]	και
angry	[thimoménos,-i,-o]	θυμωμένος,-η,-ο
another	[álos,-i,-o]	άλλος,-η,-ο
apartment building (f)	[polikatikía]	πολυκατοικία
apartment/flat (n)	[dhiamérizma]	διαμέρισμα
appetizer, starter (n)	[orektikó]	ορεκτικό
April (m)	[aprílios]	Απρίλιος
architect (m/f)	[arhitéktonas]	αρχιτέκτονας
area (m)	[hóros]	χώρος
armchair (f)	[polithróna]	πολυθρόνα
around, about	[ghíro]	γύρω
arrive	[ftháno]	φθάνω
as	[ópos]	όπως
Athens (f)	[athína]	Αθήνα
August (m)	[ávghustos]	Αύγουστος
Australia (f)	[afstralía]	Αυστραλία
autumn / fall (n)	[fthinóporo]	φθινόπωρο
availability (f)	[dhiathesimótita]	διαθεσιμότητα

B		
baby (n)	[moró]	μωρό
baby boy (m)	[bébis]	μπέμπης
baby girl (f)	[béba]	μπέμπα

balcony/porch (n)	[balkóni]	μπαλκόνι
banana (f)	[banána]	μπανάνα
bank (f)	[trápeza]	τράπεζα
basement (n)	[ipóghion]	υπόγειον
basket ball (n)	[básket]	μπάσκετ
bass (n)	[lavráki]	λαβράκι
bathroom (n)	[bánio]	μπάνιο
bathroom, toilet (f)	[tualéta]	τουαλέτα
bathtub (f)	[baniéra]	μπανιέρα
be	[íme]	είμαι
be able	[boró]	μπορώ
because	[yatí]	γιατί
be glad	[hérome]	χαίρομαι
be happy	[héro]	χαίρω
be interested	[endhiaférome]	ενδιαφέρομαι
be pleased	[héro]	χαίρω
beach (f)	[plaz]	πλαz
bean (n)	[fasóli]	φασόλι
beautiful, nice	[oréos, -a, -o]	ωραίος, -α, -ο
bed (n)	[kreváti]	κρεβάτι
bedroom (f)	[krevatokámara]	κρεβατοκάμαρα
bedroom (n)	[ipnodhomátio]	υπνοδωμάτιο
beef	[mosharísios,-a,-o]	μοσχαρίσιος,-α,-ο
beefsteak (n)	[biftéki]	μπιφτέκι
beer (f)	[bíra]	μπύρα
behind	[píso]	πίσω
beige	[bez]	μπεz
bell (n)	[kudhúni]	κουδούνι
Berlin (n)	[verolíno]	Βερολίνο
between	[metaxí]	μεταξύ
beverage, drink (n)	[potó]	ποτό
big, large	[meghálos, -i, -o]	μεγάλος, -η, -ο
bill (m)	[loghariazmós]	λογαριασμός
black	[mávros, -i, -o]	μαύρος, -η, -ο
block (n)	[tetrághono]	τετράγωνο
blue	[ble]	μπλε
blues (music) (n)	[bluz]	μπλουz
boat (f)	[várka]	βάρκα
book (n)	[vivlío]	βιβλίο
book store (n)	[vivliopolío]	βιβλιοπωλείο
booklet (n)	[filádhio]	φυλλάδιο

bottle (n)	[bukáli]	μπουκάλι
bottled	[emfialoménos]	εμφιαλωμένος
bouzouki (n)	[buzúki]	μπουζούκι
boy (n)	[aghóri]	αγόρι
bravo	[brávo]	μπράβο
bread (n)	[psomí]	ψωμί
breakfast (n)	[proinó]	πρωινό
bridge (f)	[ghéfira]	γέφυρα
brother (m)	[adhelfós]	αδελφός
brown	[kafé]	καφέ
bus (n)	[leoforío]	λεωφορείο
busy	[apasholiménos]	απασχολημένος
but	[alá]	αλλά
but	[ma]	μα
butter (n)	[vútiro]	βούτυρο

C cafe (f)	[kafetéria]	καφετέρια
can	[boró]	μπορώ
can/tin (n)	[kutí]	κουτί
car (n)	[aftokínito]	αυτοκίνητο
car park (n)	[párkin]	πάρκιν
card (f)	[kárta]	κάρτα
carrot (n)	[karóto]	καρότο
cash desk (n)	[tamío]	ταμείο
cashier's	[tamío]	ταμείο
celery (n)	[sélino]	σέλινο
central	[kendrikós, -í, -ó]	κεντρικός, ή, ό
centre/center (n)	[kéndro]	κέντρο
century (m)	[eónas]	αιώνας
cereal (n/pl)	[dhimitriaká]	δημητριακά
chair (f)	[karékla]	καρέκλα
changing room (n)	[dhokimastírio]	δοκιμαστήριο
cheap	[fthinós, -í, -ó]	φθηνός, -ή, -ό
check	[exetázo]	εξετάζω
checked (m/f/n)	[karó]	καρώ
cheque/check (f)	[epitaghí]	επιταγή
child (n)	[pedhí]	παιδί
church (f)	[eklisía]	εκκλησία
cigarette (n)	[tsigháro]	τσιγάρο
cinema (n)	[sinemá]	σινεμά
close to	[kondá]	κοντά

closed	[klistós, -í, -ó]	κλειστός, ή, ό
closet/wardrobe (f)	[dulápa]	ντουλάπα
coca cola (f)	[kóka kóla]	κόκα κόλα
coffee (m)	[kafés]	καφές
coffee house (n)	[kafenío]	καφενείο
coffee with some sugar	[métrios]	μέτριος
coffee with much sugar	[ghlikós]	γλυκός
coffee without sugar (m)	[skétos]	σκέτος
colour/color (n)	[hróma]	χρώμα
comedy (f)	[komodhía]	κωμωδία
company (f)	[etería]	εταιρεία
computer (n)	[kompiúter]	κομπιούτερ
conservatory (f)	[tzamaría]	τζαμαρία
contrast, antithesis (f)	[antíthesi]	αντίθεση
cook	[maghirévo]	μαγειρεύω
cooked foods (n/pl)	[maghireftá]	μαγειρευτά
corner (f)	[ghonía]	γωνία
counter (m)	[pángos]	πάγκος
courgette, zucchini (n)	[kolokitháki]	κολοκυθάκι
cousin (f)	[(e)xathélfi]	(ε)ξαδέλφη
cousin (m)	[(e)xáthelfos]	(ε)ξάδελφος
credit card (f)	[pistotiki kárta]	πιστωτική κάρτα
creme caramel (n)	[krem karamelé]	κρεμ καραμελέ
croissant (n)	[kruasán]	κρουασάν
cucumber (n)	[angúri]	αγγούρι
cup (n)	[flitzáni]	φλυτζάνι
currency (n)	[nómizma]	νόμισμα
customs (n)	[telonío]	τελωνείο
cutlet (f)	[brizóla]	μπριζόλα

D

dark	[skúros, -a, -o]	σκούρος, -α, -ο
date (f)	[imerominía]	ημερομηνία
daughter (f)	[kóri]	κόρη
day (f)	[(i)méra]	(η)μέρα
December (m)	[dhekémvrios]	Δεκέμβριος
deposit	[prokatavolí]	προκαταβολή
dessert (n)	[ghlikó]	γλυκό
dialogue/dialog (m)	[dhiáloghos]	διάλογος
difficult	[dhískolos, -i, -o]	δύσκολος, -η, -ο
dill (m)	[ánithos]	άνιθος
dining room (f)	[trapezaría]	τραπεζαρία

dinner (n)	[vradhinó]	βραδινό
disagree	[dhiafonó]	διαφωνώ
discotheque (f)	[dhiskothíki]	δισκοθήκη
dislike	[antipathó]	αντιπαθώ
doctor (m/f)	[yatrós]	γιατρός
door (f)	[pórta]	πόρτα
dorado or gillhead (f)	[tsipúra]	τσιπούρα
double room (n)	[dhíklino]	δίκλινο
down	[káto]	κάτω
drachma (f)	[dhrahmí]	δραχμή
dress (n)	[fórema]	φόρεμα
drink	[píno]	πίνω

E

early	[norís]	νωρίς
easy	[éfkolos, -i, -o]	εύκολος, -η, -ο
eat	[tró-o]	τρώω
eight	[októ] / [ohtó]	οκτώ / οχτώ
eight hundred	[oktakósia]	οκτακόσια
eighteen	[dhekaoktó]	δεκαοκτώ
eighty	[ogdhónda]	ογδόντα
eleven	[éndeka]	έντεκα
England (f)	[anglía]	Αγγλία
English (language) (n/pl)	[angliká]	Αγγλικά
entrance (f)	[ísodhos]	είσοδος
envelope (m)	[fákelos]	φάκελος
Euro	[evró]	ευρώ
evening (n)	[vrádhi]	βράδυ
every	[káthe]	κάθε
everything/all	[óla]	όλα
everywhere	[pandú]	παντού
exactly	[akrivós]	ακριβώς
excuse me	[sighnómi]	συγνώμη
excuse me/pardon me	[me sinhoríte]	με συγχωρείτε
exit (f)	[éxodhos]	έξοδος

F

fall/autumn	[fthinóporo]	φθινόπωρο
fall	[péfto]	πέφτω
family (f)	[ikoghénia]	οικογένεια
father (m)	[patéras]	πατέρας
February (m)	[fevruários]	Φεβρουάριος
ferryboat (n)	[féribot]	φέρυμποτ

fifteen	[dhekapénde]	δεκαπέντε
fifth	[pémptos, -i, -o]	πέμπτος, -η, -ο
fifty	[penínda]	πενήντα
film (n)	[érgho] [film]	έργο / φιλμ
finally	[teliká]	τελικά
finish	[telióno]	τελειώνω
first	[prótos, -i, -o]	πρώτος, -η, -ο
fish (n)	[psári]	ψάρι
fish restaurant (f)	[psarotavérna]	ψαροταβέρνα
five	[pénde]	πέντε
five hundred	[pendakósia]	πεντακόσια
flat, apartment (n)	[dhiamérizma]	διαμέρισμα
flight (f)	[ptísi]	πτήση
floor (m)	[orófos]	όροφος
flying dolphin,	[iptámeno dhelphíni]	ιπτάμενο δελφίνι
food cooked in oil	[ladherá]	λαδερά
football (n)	[podhósfero]	ποδόσφαιρο
for	[yá]	για
fork (n)	[pirúni]	πηρούνι
fortnight (n)	[dhekapenthímero]	δεκαπενθήμερο
forty	[saránda]	σαράντα
four	[téseris, -is, -a]	τέσσερις, -ις, -α
four hundred	[tetrakósia]	τετρακόσια
fourteen	[dhekatéseris/a]	δεκατέσσερις / α
fourth	[tétartos, -i, -o]	τέταρτος, -η, -ο
France (f)	[ghalía]	Γαλλία
free	[eléftheros, -i, -o]	ελεύθερος, -η, -ο
French (language) (n/pl)	[ghaliká]	γαλλικά
friend (m) friend (f)	[fílos] [fíli]	φίλος / φίλη
from	[apó]	από
front	[brostá]	μπροστά
fruit (n)	[frúto]	φρούτο
garage (n)	[garáz]	γκαράζ
garlic (n)	[skórdho]	σκόρδο
German (language) (n/pl)	[ghermaniká]	γερμανικά
Germany (f)	[ghermanía]	Γερμανία
get up	[sikónome]	σηκώνομαι
girl (n)	[korítsi]	κορίτσι
glass (n)	[potíri]	ποτήρι
go	[páo]	πάω

English	Pronunciation	Greek
go for a walk	[páo vólta]	πάω βόλτα
good	[kalá]	καλά
good	[kalós, -í, -ó]	καλός, -ή, -ό
good evening	[kalispéra]	καλησπέρα
good morning	[kaliméra]	καλημέρα
good night	[kaliníhta]	καληνύχτα
grandchild (n)	[egóni]	εγγόνι
granddaughter (f)	[egoní]	εγγονή
grandfather (m)	[papús]	παπούς
grandmother (f)	[yayá]	γιαγιά
grandson (m)	[egonós]	εγγονός
grape (n)	[stafíli]	σταφύλι
Greece (f)	[eládha]	Ελλάδα
Greek (language) (n/pl)	[eliniká]	ελληνικά
Greek blues (n/pl)	[rebétika]	ρεμπέτικα
Greek coffee (m)	[elinikós kafés]	ελληνικός καφές
Greek pastry (m)	[baklavás]	μπακλαβάς
Greek pastry (n)	[kataífi]	καταΐφι
Greek tavern (f)	[tavérna]	ταβέρνα
green	[prásinos, -i, -o]	πράσινος, -η, -ο
grilled foods (n/pl)	[psitá]	ψητά
ground floor (n)	[isóghion]	ισόγειον

H		
half	[misós, -í, -ó]	μισός, -ή, -ό
hallway (n)	[hol]	χωλ
hand basin (m)	[niptíras]	νιπτήρας
happy	[eftihizménos -i, -o]	ευτυχισμένος, -η, -ο
have	[ého]	έχω
he	[aftós]	αυτός
heating (f)	[thérmansi]	θέρμανση
hello / good bye	[hérete]	χαίρετε (pl/fml)
hello / goodbye	[yásas]	γεια σας (pl/fml)
hello / see you	[yásu]	γεια σου (infml)
her	[tis]	της
herb (n)	[baharikó]	μπαχαρικό
here	[edhó]	εδώ
here you are!	[oríste]	ορίστε
hi	[yásu]	γεια σου
his	[tu]	του
hobby (n)	[hóbi]	χόμπυ
homemade	[spitikós, -í, -ó]	σπιτικός, -η, -ο

hospital (n)	[nosokomío]	νοσοκομείο
hotel (n)	[xenodhohío]	ξενοδοχείο
house/home (n)	[spíti]	σπίτι
how/what	[pos]	πώς
hungry	[pinazménos, -i, -o]	πεινασμένος, -η, -ο
husband/wife (m/f)	[sízighos]	σύζυγος

I	[eghó]	εγώ
I am	[íme]	είμαι
I'm sorry/excuse me	[sighnómi]	συγνώμη
iced coffee/frappe (m)	[frapés]	φραπές
idea (f)	[idhéa]	ιδέα
immediately	[amésos]	αμέσως
in	[se]	σε
information (f)	[pliroforía]	πληροφορία
instant coffee (m)	[nes kafé]	νες καφέ
interesting	[endhiaféron]	ενδιαφέρον
introduce	[sistíno]	συστήνω
Ireland (f)	[irlandhía]	Ιρλανδία
island music (n/pl)	[nisiótika]	νησιώτικα
it	[aftó]	αυτό
Italian (language) (n/pl)	[italiká]	ιταλικά
Italy (f)	[italía]	Ιταλία
its	[tu]	του

January (m)	[ianuários]	Ιανουάριος
jazz music (f)	[tzaz]	τζαζ
job / work (f)	[dhuliá]	δουλειά
juice (m)	[himós]	χυμός
July (m)	[iúlios]	Ιούλιος
June (m)	[iúnios]	Ιούνιος

kilo (n)	[kiló]	κιλό
kiosk (n)	[periptero]	περίπτερο
kitchen (f)	[kuzína]	κουζίνα
knife(n)	[mahéri]	μαχαίρι
know	[xéro]	ξέρω

lamb (n)	[arnáki]	αρνάκι
late	[arghá]	αργά
lawn / grass (n)	[grasídhi]	γρασίδι

learn	[mathéno]	μαθαίνω
leave	[févgho]	φεύγω
left	[aristerá]	αριστερά
lemonade (f)	[lemonádha]	λεμονάδα
letter (n)	[ghráma]	γράμμα
lettuce (n)	[marúli]	μαρούλι
lift/elevator (n)	[asansér]	ασανσέρ
light (n)	[fos]	φως
light (colour), open	[aniktós, -í, -ó]	ανοικτός, ή, ό
like	[m'arési]	μ'αρέσει
likely, probably	[pithanós]	πιθανώς
little	[líghos, -i, -o]	λίγος, -n, -o
live	[méno]	μένω
living room (f)	[salóni]	σαλόνι
London (n)	[londhíno]	Λονδίνο
love story (f)	[istoría aghápis]	ιστορία αγάπης
lucky	[tiherós, -i, -ó]	τυχερός, ή, ό
luggage (f)	[aposkeví]	αποσκευή
lunch (n)	[mesimerianó]	μεσημεριανό
lyre (f)	[líra]	λύρα

M

Madrid (f)	[madhríti]	Μαδρίτη
mainly	[kiríos]	κυρίως
man / husband (m)	[ándras]	άνδρας
map (m)	[hártis]	χάρτης
March (m)	[mártios]	Μάρτιος
market (f)	[aghorá]	αγορά
marmalade (f)	[marmeládha]	μαρμελάδα
May (m)	[máios]	Μάϊος
may / is possible to	[borí na]	μπορεί να
me (after a preposition)	[(e)ména]	(ε)μένα
me (before a verb)	[mu]	μου
medium, middle	[meséos, -a, -o]	μεσαίος, -α, -ο
melon (n)	[pepóni]	πεπόνι
mezzanine (m)	[imiórofos]	ημιόροφος
midday / afternoon (n)	[mesiméri]	μεσημέρι
milk (n)	[ghála]	γάλα
minute (n)	[leptó]	λεπτό
mirror (m)	[kathréftis]	καθρέφτης
Miss	[dhespinídha]	δεσποινίδα
mixed Greek salad	[horiátiki saláta]	χωριάτικη σαλάτα

moment (n)	[leptó]	λεπτό
moment (f)	[stighmí]	στιγμή
month (m)	[mínas]	μήνας
more	[pio]	πιο
more	[perisóteros, -i, -o]	περισσότερος,-η,-ο
morning (n)	[proí]	πρωί
mother (f)	[mitéra]	μητέρα
motorcycle (f)	[motosikléta]	μοτοσυκλέτα
mountain (n)	[vunó]	βουνό
Mr./Sir	[kírios]	κύριος
Mrs./Madam/Ms.	[kiría]	κυρία
much/very	[polís, -í, -í]	πολύς, -ή, ύ
museum (n)	[musío]	μουσείο
mushroom (n)	[manitári]	μανιτάρι
music (f)	[musikí]	μουσική
musician (m/f)	[musikós]	μουσικός
must/have to	[prepi na]	πρέπει να
my	[mu]	μου

N

name (n)	[ónoma]	όνομα
national	[ethnikós, -í, -ó]	εθνικός, -ή, ό
naturally	[fisiká]	φυσικά
naught / zero	[midhén]	μηδέν
near, close to	[kondá]	κοντά
need	[hriázome]	χρειάζομαι
neighborhood (f)	[ghitoniá]	γειτονιά
never	[poté]	ποτέ
New York (f)	[néa iórki]	Νέα Υόρκη
newspaper (f)	[efimerídha]	εφημερίδα
next to	[dhípla]	δίπλα
nice, beautiful	[oréos, -a, -o]	ωραίος, -α, -ο
nice, beautiful	[ómorfos, -i, -o]	όμορφος, -η, -ο
nine	[enéa] / [eniá]	εννέα / εννιά
nine hundred	[eniakósia]	ενιακόσια
nineteen	[dhekaeniá]	δεκαεννιά
ninety	[enenínda]	ενενήντα
no	[óhi]	όχι
not	[dhen]	δεν
nothing	[típota]	τίποτα
novel (f)	[nuvéla]	νουβέλα
novel (n)	[mithistórima]	μυθιστόρημα

November (m)	[noémvrios]	Νοέμβριος
now	[tóra]	τώρα
number, size (n)	[número]	νούμερο
nurse (f)	[nosokóma]	νοσοκόμα
nurse (m)	[nosokómos]	νοσοκόμος

O October (m)

October (m)	[októvrios]	Οκτώβριος
of course, naturally	[vévea]	βέβαια
often	[sihná]	συχνά
oh	[ah]	αχ
OK, all right	[kalá] [endáxi]	καλά / εντάξει
Olympic Airways (f)	[olimbiakí]	Ολυμπιακή
one	[énas], [mía], [éna]	ένας, μία, ένα
one hundred	[ekató]	εκατό
one thousand (f)	[hílies]	χίλιες
one thousand (m)	[hílji]	χίλιοι
one thousand (n)	[hília]	χίλια
one-family house (f)	[monokatikía]	μονοκατοικία
orange (fruit)	[portokáli]	πορτοκάλι
orange (colour)	[portokalí]	πορτοκαλί
orange drink (f)	[portokaládha]	πορτοκαλάδα
our	[mas]	μας
out, outside	[éxo]	έξω
ouzo (n)	[úzo]	ούζο
oven (m)	[fúrnos]	φούρνος
over	[péra]	πέρα

P p.m.

p.m.	[metá mesimvría]	μ.μ.
pair (n)	[zevghári]	ζευγάρι
Paris (n)	[parísi]	Παρίσι
parsley (m)	[maindanós]	μαϊντανός
passport (n)	[dhiavatírio]	διαβατήριο
pear (n)	[ahládhi]	αχλάδι
penthouse (n)	[retiré]	ρετιρέ
petrol/gas (f).	[venzíni]	βενζίνη
petrol/gas station (n)	[pratírio venzínis]	πρατήριο βενζίνης
pharmacy (n)	[farmakío]	φαρμακείο
pianist (f)	[pianístria]	πιανίστρια
pianist (m)	[pianístas]	πιανίστας
pineapple (m)	[ananás]	ανανάς
pink	[roz]	ροz

plate (n)	[piáto]	πιάτο
play	[pézo]	παίζω
please (you're welcome)	[parakaló]	παρακαλώ
police (f)	[astinomía]	αστυνομία
pop music (n/pl)	[laiká]	λαϊκά
pork (n)	[hirinó]	χοιρινό
portion (f)	[merídha]	μερίδα
post office (n)	[tahidhromío]	ταχυδρομείο
potato (f)	[patáta]	πατάτα
pound (f)	[líra]	λίρα
practical	[praktikós, -í, -ó]	πρακτικός, ή, ό
prefer	[m' arési]	μ' αρέσει
prefer	[protimó]	προτιμώ
prepare	[etimázo]	ετοιμάζω
price (f)	[timí]	τιμή
private	[idhiotikós -í, -ó],	ιδιωτικός, -ή, -ό
problem (n)	[próvlima]	πρόβλημα
prospectus (n)	[prospéktus]	προσπέκτους
purple	[mov]	μωβ

Q question (f)   [erótisi]   ερώτηση

R
radio (n)	[radhiófono]	ραδιόφωνο
rain (f)	[vrohí]	βροχή
rarely	[spánia]	σπάνια
read	[dhiavázo]	διαβάζω
realize	[vlépo]	βλέπω
reception (f)	[ipodhohí]	υποδοχή
red	[kókinos, -i, -o]	κόκκινος, -η, -ο
red mullet (n)	[barbúni]	μπαρμπούνι
reservation (f)	[krátisi]	κράτηση
residence (f)	[katikía]	κατοικία
restaurant (n)	[estiatório]	εστιατόριο
return	[epistréfo]	επιστρέφω
return / round trip (f)	[epistrofí]	επιστροφή
right (direction)	[dhexiá]	δεξιά
right (n)	[dhíkio]	δίκιο
river (m)	[potamós]	ποταμός
rock (m)	[vráhos]	βράχος
rock (music) (n)	[rok]	ροκ
room (n)	[dhomátio]	δωμάτιο

round (shape)	[strongilós, -i, -o]	στρογγυλός, ή, ό
run	[tého]	τρέχω
running (n)	[trohádhin]	τροχάδην

sad	[lipiménos, -i, -o]	λυπημένος, -η, -ο
salad (f)	[saláta]	σαλάτα
sale / discount (f)	[ékptosi]	έκπτωση
same	[ídhios, -a, -o]	ίδιος, -α, -ο
Saturday (n)	[sávato]	Σάββατο
saucer (n)	[piatáki]	πιατάκι
school (n)	[sholío]	σχολείο
science (f)	[epístimi]	επιστήμη
Scotland (f)	[skotía] Σκοτία	
sea (f)	[thálasa]	θάλασσα
seaside (f)	[paralía]	παραλία
season (f)	[epohí]	εποχή
second (not minute)	[dhéfteros, -i, -o]	δεύτερος, -η, -ο
second (n)	[dhefterólepto]	δευτερόλεπτο
see	[vlépo]	βλέπω
see again	[xanavlépo]	ξαναβλέπω
September (m)	[septémvrios]	Σεπτέμβριος
sesame bread (n)	[kulúri]	κουλούρι
seven	[eptá]/[eftá]	επτά/εφτά
seven hundred	[eptakósia]	επτακόσια
seven hundred	[eftakósia]	εφτακόσια
seventeen	[dhekaeftá]	δεκαεφτά
seventy	[evdhomínda]	εβδομήντα
shampoo (n)	[sampuán]	σαμπουάν
she	[aftí]	αυτή
ship (n)	[plío]	πλοίο
shirt (n)	[pukámiso]	πουκάμισο
shoe (n)	[papútsi]	παπούτσι
shoe lace (n)	[kordhóni]	κορδόνι
shop window (f)	[vitrína]	βιτρίνα
shower (n)	[duz]	ντους
side (f)	[plevrá]	πλευρά
single room (n)	[monóklino]	μονόκλινο
sister (f)	[adhelfí]	αδελφή
sit	[káthome]	κάθομαι
sitting room (n)	[kathistikó]	καθιστικό
six	[éxi]	έξι

six hundred	[exakósia]	εξακόσια
sixteen	[dhekaéxi]	δεκαέξι
sixty	[exínda]	εξήντα
size (n)	[mégethos]	μέγεθος
sky blue	[ghalázios, -a, -o]	γαλάζιος, -α, -ο
sleep	[kimáme]	κοιμάμαι
slip-ons (loafers) (n)	[pandoflé]	παντοφλέ
slipper (f)	[pandófla]	παντόφλα
small	[mikrós, -í, -ó]	μικρός, ή, ό
small bouzouki (n)	[baghlamadháki]	μπαγλαμαδάκι
small dishes, tidbits	[mezédhes]	μεζέδες
smoke	[kapnízo]	καπνίζω
smoking (n)	[kápnizma]	κάπνισμα
so	[étsi]	έτσι
so	[tósos, -i, -o]	τόσος, -η, -ο
soap (n)	[sapúni]	σαπούνι
soda water (f)	[sódha]	σόδα
sofa (m)	[kanapés]	καναπές
soft pop (n/pl)	[elafrolaiká]	ελαφρολαϊκά
son (m)	[yos]	γιος
soup (f)	[súpa]	σούπα
soup spoon (n)	[kutáli]	κουτάλι
space, area (m)	[hóros]	χώρος
Spain (f)	[ispanía]	Ισπανία
Spanish (language)	[ispaniká]	ισπανικά
speak	[miláo]	μιλάω
sport (n)	[spor]	σπορ
spring (f)	[ánixi]	ανοίξη
stamp (n)	[ghramatósimo]	γραμματόσημο
stay	[káthome] [méno]	κάθομαι / μένω
stay (f)	[dhiamoní]	διαμονή
stay (f)	[paramoní]	παραμονή
still/yet	[akóma]	ακόμα
stool (n)	[skambó]	σκαμπό
story / history (f)	[istoría]	ιστορία
straight	[efthía]	ευθεία
straight ahead	[efthía brostá]	ευθεία μπροστά
straight ahead	[ísia]	ίσια
strawberry (f)	[fráula]	φράουλα
striped (m/f/n)	[righé]	ριγέ
studio / bedsit (f)	[garsoniéra]	γκαρσονιέρα

study	[dhiavázo]	διαβάζω
study	[mathéno]	μαθαίνω
stuffed peppers	[ghemistá]	γεμιστά
stuffed tomatoes	[ghemistá]	γεμιστά
suitcase (f)	[valítsa]	βαλίτσα
summer (n)	[kalokéri]	καλοκαίρι
Sunday (f)	[kiriakí]	Κυριακή
supermarket (n)	[supermárket]	σούπερμαρκετ
sure!	[amé]!	αμέ!
surprised	[ékpliktos, -i, -o]	έκπληκτος, -η, -ο
sweet	[ghlikos, -iá, ó]	γλυκός, -ιά, -ό
Sydney (n)	[sídhnei]	Σίδνεϋ

T table (n)	[trapézi]	τραπέζι
table tennis (n)	[ping pong]	πινκ πονκ
take	[pérno]	παίρνω
taverna	[tavérna]	ταβέρνα
taxi (n)	[taxí]	ταξί
tea (n)	[tsái]	τσάϊ
tea spoon (n)	[kutaláki]	κουταλάκι
teacher (f)	[dhaskála]	δασκάλα
teacher (m)	[dháskalos]	δάσκαλος
telephone (n)	[tiléfono]	τηλέφωνο
telephone call (n)	[tilefónima]	τηλεφώνημα
television (f)	[tileórasi]	τηλεόραση
ten	[dhéka]	δέκα
tennis (n)	[ténis]	τένις
thanks [lit. I thank you]	[efharistó]	ευχαριστώ
thanks [lit. we thank you]	[efharistúme]	ευχαριστούμε
that / who (in statements)	[pu]	που
the (m, f, n)	[o], [i], [to]	ο, η, το
theatre (n)	[théatro]	θέατρο
their	[tus]	τους
then, afterwards	[metá]	μετά
then / after that / later	[épita]	έπειτα
there	[ekí]	εκεί
Thessaloniki (f)	[thesaloníki]	Θεσσαλονίκη
they (only females)	[aftés]	αυτές
they (only males)	[aftí]	αυτοί
they (males and females)	[aftí]	αυτοί
they (only things)	[aftá]	αυτά

thing	[prághma]	πράγμα
think	[nomízo]	νομίζω
third	[trítos, -i, -o]	τρίτος, -η, -ο
thirsty	[dhipsazménos]	διψασμένος
thirteen	[dhekatrís, -ís, -ía]	δεκατρείς, -ίς, -ία
thirty	[triánda]	τριάντα
though, although	[ómos]	όμως
three (m-f-n)	[trís, trís, tría]	τρεις, τρεις, τρία
three hundred	[trakósia]	τριακόσια
thriller / horror (n)	[thríler]	θρίλερ
ticket (n)	[isitírio]	εισπτήριο
time (f)	[óra]	ώρα
time (m)	[hrónos]	χρόνος
time (m)	[kerós]	καιρός
tired (m, f)	[kurazménos, -i]	κουρασμένος, -η
tiring	[kurastikós, -í, -ó]	κουραστικός, -ή, -ό
to (used with verbs)	[na]	να
to (preposition)	[ston], [stin], [sto]	στον, στην, στο
to, until	[méhri]	μέχρι
today (n)	[símera]	σήμερα
toilet (f)	[tualéta]	τουαλέτα
tomato (f)	[domáta]	ντομάτα
toothbrush (f)	[odhondóvurtsa]	οδοντόβουρτσα
toothpaste (f)	[odhondópasta]	οδοντόπαστα
towel (f)	[petséta]	πετσέτα
town / city (f)	[póli]	πόλη
train (n)	[tréno]	τρένο
train station (m)	[stathmós trénon]	σταθμός τρένων
travel	[taxidhi]	ταξίδι
trip (n)	[taxídhi]	ταξίδι
triple room (n)	[tríklino]	τρίκλινο
trout (f)	[péstrofa]	πέστροφα
truth (f)	[alíthia]	αλήθεια
twelve	[dhódheka]	δώδεκα
twenty	[íkosi]	είκοσι
two	[dhío]	δύο
two hundred	[dhiakósia]	διακόσια
tzatziki (n)	[tzatzíki]	τζατζίκι
underground (n)	[metró]	μετρό
understand	[vlépo]	βλέπω

understand	[katalavéno]	καταλαβαίνω
unfortunately	[dhistihós]	δυστυχώς
until	[méhri]	μέχρι
until	[óspu]	ώσπου
up	[páno]	πάνω
upset	[taraghménos, -i, -o]	ταραγμένος, -η, -ο
usually	[siníthos]	συνήθως

V vegetable (n)	[lahanikó]	λαχανικό
view (f)	[théa]	θέα
volley ball (n)	[vólei]	βόλεϋ

W W.C. (n)	[vesé]	W.C.
wait	[periméno]	περιμένω
waiter	[servitóros]	σερβιτόρος
waitress	[servitóra]	σερβιτόρα
wake up	[xipnáo]	ξυπνάω
Wales (f)	[ualía]	Ουαλία
walk	[perpató]	περπατώ
walk, stroll, car ride (f)	[vólta]	βόλτα
want	[thélo]	θέλω
watch	[vlépo]	βλέπω
watch (n)	[rolói]	ρολόι
water (n)	[neró]	νερό
we	[emís]	εμείς
weather (m)	[kerós]	καιρός
week (f)	[evdhomádha]	εβδομάδα
weekend (n)	[savatokíriako]	Σαββατοκύριακο
well (e.g. I'm well)	[kalá]	καλά
well (e.g. well, what?)	[lipón]	λοιπόν
what / how	[ti]	τι
when (in questions)	[póte]	πότε
when	[ótan]	όταν
where	[pu]	πού
white	[áspros, -i, -o]	άσπρος, -η, -ο
why	[yatí]	γιατί
window (n)	[paráthiro]	παράθυρο
wine (n)	[krasí]	κρασί
winter (m)	[himónas]	χειμώνας
woman / wife (f)	[ghinéka]	γυναίκα
work	[dhulévo]	δουλεύω

work (f)	[dhuliá]	δουλειά
world (m)	[kózmos]	κόσμος
write	[ghráfo]	γράφω
writer (m/f)	[sighraféas]	συγγραφέας
yard (f)	[avlí]	αυλή
year (m)	[hrónos]	χρόνος
yellow	[kítrinos, -i, -o]	κίτρινος, -η, -o
yes	[ne]	ναι
Yes, sure! Of course!	[málista]	μάλιστα
you (pl/fml)	[esís]	εσείς
you (pl/fml)	[sas]	σας
you (sing)	[esí]	εσύ
you're welcome	[parakaló]	παρακαλώ
your (pl/fml)	[sas]	σας
your (sing/infml)	[su]	σου

www.

Books, etc...

162

Further reading

This section includes some recommendations for the traveler who is interested in learning something about the history, life, and culture of the Greek people. It is not by any means an exhaustive list but it will assist most of us who... run out of time! We have separated our ideas into real books for the... armchair traveler and electronic sites for the IT-inclined ones! Our recommendations have excluded thick, scholarly tomes; they are rather easy, pleasant reading for the layman.

A

www: The most important sites about Greece and the Greek language! Are you connected? So much the better!

B

Books, etc...

www: The most important sites about Greece and the Greek language! Are you connected? So much the better!

There are numerous websites to help you enjoy and understand the Greek language and culture. Some are bilingual, some only in Greek. Here you go:

▦ Cultural heritage

www.greece.gr is a sophisticated online magazine about Greece. www.culture.gr is the website of the Ministry of Culture and hosts many of the country's museums. www.reconstructions.org has fabulous 3-D models of the Parthenon. www.fhw.gr is the website of the Foundation of the Hellenic World. www.pbs.org/empires/thegreeks brings Ancient Greece alive. www.sae.gr is the site of the World Council of Hellenes abroad. www.ime.gr and www.hellenic-cosmos.gr will connect you to the Foundation for Greater Hellenism.

▦ Transport

www.gtp.gr gives ferry timetables. www.ose.gr offers train information. www.ktel.gr gives bus timetables and routes. www.aia.gr is the website for the new Athens airport. www.olympic-airways.gr, www.airmanos.gr, www.cronus.gr, or www.airgreece.gr offer domestic flight information.

▦ Travel

www.greekholidays.com/cities_and_islands.html is a website about travel and holidays in Greece. The Greek National Tourism Organization can be found under www.gnto.gr. You can also access www.travelling.gr or www.greekislands.gr for travel agencies, tourist offices and tourist attractions. www.ntua.gr/weather offers frequently updated information on the weather.

▦ Greek language

Information about online Greek language courses can be obtained from polyglot24@hotmail.com. If you are interested in Greek poetry in English, send an e-mail to poetrygreece@hotmail.com. Writing to centre@greeklanguage.gr will connect you to the Greek Language Center of the Ministry of Education which can offer valuable information about Greek classes or language examinations. www.cyathens.org is a study-abroad-programme of the College Year in Athens.

▦ Miscellaneous

www.greekcuisine.com offers an extensive array of Greek recipes. www.greekwine.gr lists several Greek wines from all over Greece. There are two daily newspapers in English: www.k-english.com and ww.athensnews.dolnet.gr. www.in.gr is the largest Greek portal on the web for Greek speakers. www.athens.olympic.org is an important site for everyone interested in the Olympic Games in Athens in 2004. www.hellasyellow.gr is the site for the Greek yellow pages. www.book.culture.gr is the site for the National Book Centre of Greece, listing many Greek books translated in English.

B Books, etc...

Finding books on Greece in English is not difficult; choosing from among them is! Go over the list... and happy reading!

▥ Travel books

There are numerous books to choose from.
We would like to give you two tips: check out the list of travel books from the publisher of this book on a separate page. It covers topics and destinations all over Greece. Pick up the free GNTO brochure "Travelling in Greece".

▥ Language books

Books from the same author of this phrase book include "Teach Yourself Beginner's Greek" and "Teach Yourself Greek - The Complete Course", both published by Hodder and Stoughton in London available from language specialist online bookstores or even from www.madaboutbooks.com the publisher's site.
Hardy's, A.D., Greek Language and People, BBC, 1983 is also a useful book for elementary Greek.

▥ History books

Campbell, John and Philip Sherrard, Modern Greece, New York, Praeger, 1968 - Clogg, R.A., A Social History of Modern Greece, New York, Cambridge University Press, 1986 - Woodhouse, C.M., Modern Greece: A "Short History", London, Faber-Faber, 1986

Book worm?

▥ If you are in Athens, check out Eleftheroudakis Bookstore on 16 Panepistimiou Str. for the largest selection on books about Greece in English.
"Ithaca: Books from Greece" which is a bimonthly magazine promoting Greek books abroad is also a good source. Contact the National Book Center, at 3-5 Sapphous Str. in Athens.

Texts: ARISTARHOS MATSUKAS
Art Editor: RANIA TSILOGIANNOPOULOU
Illustrations: FANIS SKAFIDAS - OLOGRAMMA
Illustrations' colours: STEPHANE PAITREAU

Colour Separation - Printing: M. TOUBIS EDITIONS S.A.